To

my parents, my wife, Hui-Chih, and my daughter, Lisa

ACKNOWLEDGMENTS

First of all, I would like to express my sincere gratitude to my dissertation advisor, Dr. Randy Chow, for his guidance and support, which made the completion of this work possible, and also for his philosophical advice on both my academic and nonacademic life, which made me more mature, personally and scholastically. I also want to express my thanks to Dr. Newman-Wolfe for his numerous fruitful discussions which provided deeper insights into some parts of this research. Thanks also go to Dr. Jih-Kwon Peir, Dr. Paul Fishwick, and Dr. Samuel Trickey for their many constructive questions and witty suggestions for my research work. Furthermore, I wish to thank all the department faculty who stimulated my strong interests and provided me with the methodology to explore the magic world of computer science.

Special thanks go to my parents for their continued support, emotional and financial. They always possessed great confidence in my capability through one and half years at University of Michigan and six years at University of Florida. Any endeavor of mine would have been futile without their unmatchable love.

Finally, words are never enough to express my gratitude to my beloved wife, Hui-Chih, for her constant patience, encouragement, and inspiration during the work of this dissertation, and for her unreserved devotion to the care of our family.

TABLE OF CONTENTS

LIST OF FIGURES

Abstract of Dissertation Presented to the Graduate School
of the University of Florida in Partial Fulfillment of the
Requirements for Doctor of Philosophy

EFFECTIVE AND EFFICIENT AUTHENTICATION AND AUTHORIZATION IN DISTRIBUTED SYSTEMS

By

I-Lung Kao

August 1995

Chairman: Dr. Randy Chow
Major Department: Computer and Information Science and Engineering

Distributed systems are inherently more vulnerable to security threats than single computer systems due to their openness in architecture, nonexistence of a centralized management authority, and the need for interactions across a wide range of autonomous and heterogeneous computers over open and insecure communication networks. More in-depth study and investigation into different subjects of authentication and authorization are of immediate importance to further applicability of distributed systems. This research explores various security problems and provides an innovative solution to each problem.

In the first part of this research, we concentrate on enhancing performance of authentication and key distribution protocols. A new authentication protocol based on uncertified session keys is proposed and shown to be minimum in message complexity. The protocol is refined further to counter session key compromises and extended to support repeated authentication to reduce the workload of authentication services. An extension of the protocol is performed to achieve transparent and and autonomous authentication for inter-domain applications.

The second part of this research addresses modeling of complex access control policies. Multilevel exceptions are systematically categorized, and their significance is justified by many desirable commercial security policies. A new model based on boolean expressions for classifying categories is proposed to enforce these exceptions and access sequences in a uniform manner.

Enforcement of complex security requirements using capabilities is considered in the third part of this research. The main strategy is to place tedious and complicated access control information on traditional capabilities distributed to subjects, and to equip object servers with only simple and regulated rules to process capabilities. It has been shown that many security policies which must be enforced by conventional centralized methods can now be enforced with an efficient distributed mechanism.

In summary, this dissertation is devoted to the investigation of many emerging security issues in distributed systems. Significant results have been demonstrated that efficiency and effectiveness of authentication and authorization services and mechanisms can be enhanced by evolutionary and revolutionary methodologies.

CHAPTER 1
INTRODUCTION

1.1 Computer Security

A computer system is a collection of hardware (CPU, memory, disks, I/O equipment, etc.) and data (system software, application programs, files, etc.) that an organization uses to perform computing tasks. Computer security is a concept of controlling *accesses to data* in a computer system for an organization such that only authorized users, or processes operating on behalf of them, will have rights to create, read, write, execute, delete, or perform other operations on the data, in accord with the security policies of the organization. In order to realize this concept, a secure computer system must provide a number of *security services* to its users.

1.1.1 Objectives of Computer Security

The principal objectives of computer security can be more specifically characterized as the protection of *confidentiality*, *integrity*, and *availability* of data stored in a computer system, as explained below.

- Protecting data confidentiality: preventing unauthorized viewing of data. Any data private to a user should not be revealed to other users who have no rights to read them.

1

- Protecting data integrity: preventing unauthorized modification of data. Any data modification which includes change, deletion, or creation of the names, formats, and contents of data should be performed only by authorized users.

- Protecting data availability: preventing *denial of service*. Any authorized user should not be prevented from accessing the data to which the user has a legitimate access right.

1.1.2 Computer Security Services

To achieve these computer security objectives, a secure computer system needs to provide a set of computer security services. With these services, the users can protect their data and the system can protect its resources appropriately. In general, all the security services of a computer system fall into the following three categories.

- *Authentication*: verifying the identity of a user or a process on behalf of the user, when the user logs in a computer system. In simple words, an authentication service tries to answer the question "Who are you ?".

- *Authorization*: controlling all accesses to data, according to some pre-determined security policies. In simple words, an authorization service tries to answer the question "What can you access and how ?".

- *Auditing*: recording occurrences of all security-relevant events in an audit log. In simple words, an auditing service tries to answer the question "What have you done ?".

How these services are implemented is elaborated as follows.

Authentication

The authentication service is usually the first service that a user will experience before the user can proceed to perform any other computing tasks. Since all other security services depend on the success of authentication, an authentication service must be as reliable and robust as possible. The traditional approach, still the most common one, to authenticate the identity of a user is the use of a *password*, which is a secret character string kept by both a user and the authentication service. Password security has been researched extensively and many principles of avoiding uses of weak passwords have been proposed [18, 36]. Since all user's passwords in a computer system are usually stored in a single password file, it is apparently crucial that the secrecy and integrity of the password file be fully protected. Some modern computer systems use *smart cards* [1] to authenticate users. A smart card is a device which is held by a user just like a ATM bank card. Usually it consists of a microprocessor, limited memory, and pre-implemented cryptographic algorithms. When a user logs in, the user inserts his card into a smart card reader and types a password, and a special identification string based on the information both on the smart card and from the user's input is computed and checked by the system. The main advantages of smart cards are that the authentication process is more secure than simply using user passwords (since both a smart card and a password need to be present), and a user can logs in a computer system from anywhere where there is a smart card reader (since the cryptographic algorithm and mechanism are provided by the smart card, rather than stored in the machine). More advanced authentication methods use *biometric authentication devices* [68] to recognize a user's personal characteristics like the voice, retina, or fingerprints of the user. Showing the greatest promise of authentication, biometric devices, however, need advanced speech or image processing technology, and their high costs are only justified where the benefits they provide are absolutely required.

Authorization (Access Control)

Each access of a user or a process executing on behalf of the user to some data needs to be controlled by the authorization service. To describe how data accesses should be mediated, unambiguous and well-defined *security policies* or *access control policies* must be described, which consists of a set of rules used by the system to determine whether an access attempt by a user to some specific data should be granted or denied. A *security model* or *access control model* is a formal representation (by mathematical notations and formalisms) used to enforce the security policies of a system. A security model provides a conceptual means to depict how each data access can be regulated by the authorization service. Note that a security policy is defined to reflect the security requirements of an organization or its users, and should be established independent of any security models. A security model describes how each access decision is determined in order not to violate the security policy. Naturally, it is desirable to choose a security model that can enforce a wide variety of security policies. However, ease of implementation and efficiency of operation of a security model are crucial to the applicability of the model.

A security model only provides an abstract way of enforcing security policies. In practice, it needs to be realized by many hardware and software features, operating functions, and management procedures, all working together to perform the activities of an authorization service. Traditionally, the authorization service is a part of the system kernel, which means security model and policies cannot be changed after the *security kernel* is constructed. Recently, a more flexible *separation of policy and mechanism* philosophy is utilized. That is, the authorization service is separated from the kernel by building a user-space authorization server to accommodate distinct security models and policies and requiring the underlying kernel mechanisms only to enforce each decision of the authorization server.

Auditing

The auditing service can be thought as the last defense line for a secure computer system. In case a security service fails or a security violation occurs, the auditing log can be reviewed and examined to reveal imperfections of security mechanisms and to trace the responsible security violators. Such traces often provides the most valuable information for improving security services of a computer system. The capability of selecting security related events to be recorded is necessary to minimize the expense of auditing and to allow efficient analysis. For obvious reasons, the audit data itself must be protected from unauthorized modification and destruction.

These three security services are indispensable for almost all computer systems. Design and implementation of these services must be taken into consideration in parallel with realization of other non-security related services (e.g., file service, print service) because of the interactions among them. The correctness, effectiveness, and efficiency of security services are apparently vital to the practicability of a computer system.

1.2 Security in Distributed Systems

Distributed systems are inherently more vulnerable to security threats than single computer systems due to their openness in architecture and their needs for interactions across a wide range of autonomous and heterogeneous systems over open and insecure communication links [16, 64, 82].

In a distributed system governed by a single administrative authority, data and resources are distributed among multiple machines and managed by different servers. A user on one machine may access data and resources on another machine by using communication primitives and networking protocols provided by the system to transfer his requests and accept responses from the remote machine. Under these circumstances, user authentication and data access control become extremely difficult to coordinate among distributed nodes. When a user tries to access data located at a remote machine, the remote data server not only may ask "who are you ?" but also needs to know "where do you come from ?", because not all remote machines are trusted or allowed to access local data. Furthermore, different servers may use incompatible access control mechanisms to enforce their security policies for the data and resource under their control. As a result, a re-interpretation of local security policies by a remote server and a translation of security mechanisms between two servers may be necessary [64].

Inter-machine communication by message passing through vulnerable network links also opens doors for security intruders. Both message confidentiality and integrity need to be achieved by cryptographic techniques applied to the data transmitted on an insecure network. Since an network intruder could masquerade as a legal user by intercepting, forging, and replaying messages on a network link, some mechanisms must be employed to guarantee *message origin authentication* [81].

In addition, distributed systems are prone to malfunction and containing unreliable components. The correctness proofs of system control algorithms and communication protocols are harder in such an environment because of its many unpredictable behaviors. Since distributed computing has become the dominant architecture of modern computer systems, a careful study of the security issues in distributed systems is of immediate and lasting importance.

CHAPTER 2
BACKGROUND AND LITERATURE SURVEY

2.1   Preamble

The research work in this dissertation falls into three main areas of computer and communications security: authentication and key distribution, access control models and policies, and capability systems. In each of these research areas, the problems found, the methods used, and the results achieved will be discussed in detail in a separate chapter. A thorough overview of previous research in these fields is given in this chapter.

2.2   Authentication and Key Distribution

In a distributed computing environment with machines connected by vulnerable network links, any two principals[1] on different machines need to authenticate each other first, on their communication initiation, such that a network intruder cannot impersonate one principal to the other by manipulating the messages transmitted over the network.

Authentication in a distributed system is usually achieved with a prudent application of cryptography and reliance upon a third-party *authentication server* which is "trusted" by all the principals in an administrative domain. The authentication

---

[1]Principal is a terminology used in authentication. A principal is a user or a process running on behalf of the user.

8

server shares a unique *master key* with each principal, and all the authentication information conveyed between the server and that principal is encrypted with the master key of that principal. To authenticate its identity to its communicating peer, a principal needs to demonstrate its ability of recognizing the authentication information encrypted with its own master key, but without revealing them (including its master key) to all other principals.

Furthermore, distributed applications frequently require that the messages transmitted over the network be confidential specifically to a pair of communicating peers (e.g., the on-line credit card payment of electronic commerce), which implies at least a *session key* needs to be distributed first between two communicating principals before a session of confidential data transmission between them can initiate. This session key is also used to provide *message origin authentication* during data communication following an authentication process. That is, any message encrypted with the session key after authentication is believed to originate from the peer principal which holds the session key. Thus, the distribution of a session key is often carried out concurrently with the authentication process.

2.2.1 Authentication Protocols

An *authentication protocol* is a communication protocol which achieves mutual authentication and key distribution between two principals communicating via networks. The first authentication protocol for networked computers was proposed by Needham and Schroeder [62]. After their pioneer work, a number of protocols with similar assumptions about the environments where the protocols are to be operated has been introduced [54]. In general, all the authentication protocols for distributed systems can be largely divided into two categories, depending upon how the freshness of key distribution messages is determined. One category of protocols uses *nonces* (a nonce is a "number used only once") and *challenge/response exchanges* to verify if the response to a key distribution request is fresh or not. Since *replay attacks* can be effectively prevented by the use of nonces, most authentication protocols proposed in the literature are nonce-based [49, 62, 63, 65, 67, 84]. The other category of protocols uses *timestamps* to ensure the freshness of messages and need to be based on the assumption that all machines involved in an authentication are properly clock-synchronized [55]. The number of messages required by timestamp-based protocols can be reduced since no round-trip traffic is required to guarantee message freshness as in the case of nonce-based protocols. However, due to the possible imperfection of clock synchronization mechanisms, timestamp-based protocols are vulnerable to both the conventional *copy-and-replay* attack and the *suppress-and-play* attack as discussed by Gong [31].

2.2.2 Repeated Authentication

After the initial authentication is established and a communication session has been completed between two principals, there may be future needs for more communication sessions between the same pair of principals. In an environment where it is reasonable to assume that the session key is not so easy to compromise, authentication for subsequent sessions can be accomplished by using *repeated authentication* to reduce the workload of the authentication server. The basic idea is to deposit some credential containing the session key of a principal at its communicating peer in an initial authentication session, and to convey the credential back to its owner in a subsequent authentication session, such that the session key earlier used can be extracted, without the need to contact with the authentication server again. Using repeated authentication prudently can effectively reduce the key generation workload of the authentication server and the corresponding communication overhead, without sacrificing the security of an authentication process. The KSL protocol proposed by Kehne, Schonwalder, and Langendorfer [49] and the Neuman-Stubblebine protocol [65] are the two most often cited authentication protocols supporting the feature of repeated authentication. Although the latter has better performance in terms of message complexity than the former, it achieves a weaker set of formalized authentication goals (see below). These two protocols will be compared further in the next chapter.

2.2.3 Formal Protocol Analysis and Evaluation

Most authentication protocols found in the literature are described only by listing the messages sent between principals and by explaining what results will be achieved after each step of message transmission, in quite an informal and imprecise way. To formalize the definition of a protocol, Burrows, Abadi, and Needham defined a logic of authentication [13] (hereafter called BAN Logic) to describe the initial assumptions upon which a protocol is based and the meaning of each message in a logical and precise way, and to express exactly what final beliefs can be obtained by communicating principals after the completion of a protocol run. The strength of BAN Logic was demonstrated by applying the logic to a number of authentication protocols and evaluating the nature of the guarantees those protocols offer. In the milestone paper introducing BAN Logic, the *formalized goals of authentication* were explicitly stated, and many protocols which could achieve these goals were appropriately criticized and improved wherever possible.

2.2.4   Design and Implementation of Authentication Services

As part of Project Athena at MIT, *Kerberos* [77] is one of the most promising implementations of authentication services. It is based on the original Needham-Schroeder protocol and uses timestamps suggested by Denning and Sacco [21] to prevent replays and to reduce messages complexity. While the initial version of Kerberos is based upon a secret-key cryptosystem (e.g., DES), a public-key cryptosystem (e.g., RSA) has been incorporated into a later version. Because of its early appearance and reliability, Kerberos has now become the most popular authentication service in industry and has been adopted as the standard security service of the Distributed Computing Environment.

In spite of its popularity and widespread acceptance, Kerberos has received its share of criticisms [8], largely addressed to the use of timestamps in the protocol. Recently, an innovative network security service called *KryptoKnight* [59] was developed by IBM Zurich Research Laboratory to avoid many problems attributed to Kerberos. KryptoKnight is designed upon the basis of a family of novel authentication and key distribution protocols which have been proved to be capable of resisting a number of *interleaving attacks* [10], and can be used in a variety of network configurations and communication paradigms. Since compactness of authentication messages is extremely enhanced by using a one-way function instead of bulk encryption as in Kerberos whenever possible, Kryptoknight can be adapted to communication protocols at any layer (e.g., by using the unused space of a TCP header), without requiring major protocol augmentation in order to accommodate security-related information. Furthermore, since the KryptoKnight protocol family is nonce-based, the security risks from improper clock synchronization in Kerberos do not come into existence.

2.3 Access Control Models and Policies

In general, access control models are divided into *mandatory* access control models and *discretionary* access control models [20, 51, 61]. Both are formulated to allow or deny particular access modes by subjects to objects[2]. In mandatory access control, each access to an object can be granted or denied to a subject based on a comparison of the security attributes associated with the object and the subject. Thus a mandatory model must contain access control rules which are imposed on all the users of a system. In discretionary access control, each access to an object can be granted or denied to any subject at the "discretion" of the owner of the object. In other words, the existence of mandatory access control in an organization's system implies that all the objects in the system belong to and are strictly controlled by the organization, but with discretionary access control, subjects are allowed to own some private objects. Both kinds of models also differ in how access authorizations are modified. With a mandatory model, authorization modifications can only be

---

[2]Subject and object are terminologies used in access control. A subject is any active entity which can request access operations, such as a user or a process running on behalf of the user. An object is any passive data storage, such as a file, a memory segment, etc.

made by system security administrators through changing the security attributes of subjects and/or objects. On the other hand, a discretionary model gives a subject some degree of freedom to pass the whole or part of its access privileges for an object to another subject.

2.3.1 Multilevel Security

The concept of multilevel security had been employed by military and government agencies for a long time before classified information was computerized. However, its significance in computer security was not really emphasized by system designers and vendors until recently. The Trusted Computer Security Evaluation Criteria (known as "the Orange Book") [61] has clearly defined multilevel security as a pre-requisite for any computer system to be classified at B1 or above. A multilevel security model is a *lattice-based* model, in the sense that each subject and object is associated with a *security class*, and the set of all possible security classes constitutes a lattice. All classes in a lattice are partially ordered by a dominance relation. The access control rules of a model reflect the model's security goal and are used to ensure that a subject can only have access, in some mode (read or write), to an object when the security class of the subject dominates or is dominated by that of the object. A security class usually includes two independent components, a hierarchical *security level* indicating the trustworthiness of a subject or the sensitivity of the information contained in an object, and a non-hierarchical *security category set*, which is purposed for implementing the *need-to-know* rule (a subject should have access privileges only to the objects which it needs to access) and uses set containment as the dominance relation. The most well-known multilevel security models are the Bell-LaPadula model [7] for data *confidentiality* and the Biba model [9] for data *integrity*. While the former concerns prevention of the unauthorized disclosure of classified and categorized information, the latter emphasizes prevention of unauthorized modification of them.

The obvious advantages of multilevel security models are easy to comprehend, simple to implement, and capable of operating with high efficiency because the authorization of an access from a subject to an object is determined simply by comparing security classes of both entities using straightforward mathematical rules, rather than by enumerating a (possibly long) access control list [24].

2.3.2 Access Control Matrix

A discretionary access control model basically enumerates all the subjects and objects in a system and regulates the access to an object based on the identity of a subject or the groups to which it belongs [61]. The most common discretionary model is the *access control matrix* defined by Harrison, Ruzzo, and Ullman [37] with a row for each subject and a column for each object. Each entry of the access control matrix, $A[i, j]$, describes the access rights that subject i has for each object j. Each object has a owner which is indicated by a "owner" right within the subject. The permission of transferring access rights for an object from a subject to another is indicated by the presence of a *transfer* right in the corresponding subject/object entry. For performance reasons, an access control matrix is usually implemented by either a row-based mechanism (*capability lists*) or a column-based mechanism (*access control lists*), and both have their own pros and cons [24]. To restrict both storage and computation overhead, many existing operating systems actually adopt a simplified (and thus less powerful) models of the HRU access control matrix. For example, UNIX divides all subject accesses into three basic domains, *self*, *group*, and *others*, and only three types of operations (read, write, execute) to each object (file) are allowed.

Due to the fact that each access authorization to an object by a subject is determined only by the identity of the subject, a computing environment with only discretionary access control may lead to unauthorized information leakage (known as *the confinement problem*) and is vulnerable to attacks by a *Trojan horse*, which is usually interpreted as pieces of hidden codes intentionally placed in a program to perform extra functions in addition to the normal goals of the program. A Trojan horse may cause dissemination of sensitive information (violating data confidentiality) or propagation of suspect information to "clean" objects (violating data integrity). On the contrary, a multilevel security model requires each object or information extracted from it to be labeled with an appropriate security class during storage and transmission, and thus the confinement property can be enforced.

2.3.3 Commercial Security Policies

Although computer security has been emphasized by military and government agencies where most information need to be classified, it did not get much attention from the commercial sector until recent years. Traditional information classification is achieved with the Bell-LaPadula multilevel security model. However, commercial applications often have radically different security requirements from multilevel security, which hence need to be enforced by other security models and mechanisms. In the following, some well-known and frequently desired commercial security policies, that are all hard to be enforced by multilevel security, are listed and described briefly [42].

- **The Clark/Wilson commercial integrity policy:** As pointed out by Clark and Wilson in their well-known paper [15], data in commercial applications is not necessarily associated with a particular security level as in the military, but rather with a set of programs permitted to manipulate it. Further, users usually are not given authority to access data directly, but to execute certain programs on certain data items. Clark and Wilson pointed out that a commercial security policy focuses on data integrity instead of confidentiality and consists of two basic concepts, *well-formed transactions* and *separation of duty*. The concept of well-formed transactions is that a user should not manipulate commercial data arbitrarily, but only in constrained ways that preserve or ensure the integrity of data. Separation of duty attempts to ensure the external consistency of data objects by separating all operations to data into several subparts and requiring that each subpart be executed by a different user. It has been claimed by Clark and Wilson and further shown by other researchers [52, 74] that a lattice-based multilevel security model is not sufficient to enforce this commercial security policy, unless a concept of *partially trusted subject* (which is a subject possessing a range of, rather than a single one, security classes) is implemented.

- **The Chinese Wall security policy:** Claimed to be "perhaps as significant to some parts of the commercial world as Bell and LaPadula's policies are to the military", the Chinese Wall security policy [12] is a concrete example of typical security requirements in the financial world. It regulates how a market analyst working for a financial institution providing corporate business service can access corporate information, such that the analyst cannot advise or give marketing information to corporations which are in competition with each other. It also has been shown that multilevel security models cannot enforce this well-known policy without resorting to extra access control mechanisms [12] .

- **The data-formatting software problem:** As desired by many transaction-type applications, raw business data are usually not permitted to be read by users directly, without being converted to a specific format by some formatting software. Some examples include a spreadsheet program with formatted tables and figures, and a database user interface with extracted and re-configured data tables. Multilevel security cannot enforce such a requirement on account of the transitivity property of a lattice. Because if raw data can be read by a formatting software which converts it to formatted data, and a user is allowed to read formatted data, then the user must be able to read raw data.

- **Specifying a sequence of accesses:** Commercial applications often have the need that a fixed sequence of accesses to a file be specified among several different types of users. An example mentioned in [72] is that a check must be prepared first by a clerk, and then approved by a supervisor, and finally bookkeeped and issued by an accountant. Such a sequence of access operations must be strictly enforced on every check. Again, a multilevel security model does not provide any tool to specify a sequence of accesses to an object.

All these commercial security policies cannot be nicely enforced by traditional multilevel security models since they originate from specific security requirements which are not directly relevant to strict information classification and categorization. In effect, security policies become more complex in a distributed computing environment, due to greater dispersal of data and more complicated access characteristics of users.

2.4   Capability Systems

Capabilities were first proposed by Dennis and Van Horn [22] as a mechanism for object addressing and access privilege representation, and later used as a fundamental access control mechanism of many operating systems [50, 53, 76, 83]. A capability used as a privilege certificate in computer systems is just like a ticket used in the human world. When a subject makes an access request to an object, a capability must be presented along with that request, and only the access operation which is also specified on the capability will be allowed.

2.4.1   User-Space and Identity-Based Capabilities

Traditional capabilities are protected from tampering by storing them in the system space and managing them only by the (trusted) kernel of an operating system. Amoeba [80] is the first distributed operating system which uses capabilities in the user space.[3] In Amoeba, all objects (files, devices, etc.) are managed by user-space object servers and a capability is presented from a subject to the object server for accessing an object under its control. Since capabilities are distributed to the user processes, a cryptographic technique is needed to prevent capability forgery. This non-system-controlled capability-based framework has now become an attractive approach to the design of modern distributed operating systems [35]. Capabilities are no longer under tight control of kernels, and instead are managed by users themselves and incorporated into the remote procedure call mechanisms for accessing objects.

A major disadvantage of traditional capabilities shown by Boebert [11] is that a classical capability system is unable to enforce the *-property of the multilevel security policy, due to the property that *"the right to exercise access carries with it the right to grant the access"*. Thus it is possible that a capability can be propagated across domains of subjects at different levels without being detected, and subsequently can cause unauthorized accesses [40]. The *ICAP* system proposed by Gong [29, 30] solves this problem by incorporating the identities of subjects into traditional capabilities, to enable the monitoring, meditating, and recording of capability propagations.

2.4.2 Capabilities in Distributed Systems

No matter what access control models are used in a computer system, practical access authorization is usually implemented by using either *access control lists* or *capability lists*, or their variations. Although both access control mechanisms have

---

[3]In fact, in a distributed system, the kernels of user machines cannot be trusted any more, so there is no point in putting capabilities in the system space.

their own advantages and disadvantages, in a distributed system capabilities are more suitable for implementation than access control lists for a number of reasons. Using a capability-based system, an object server will only need to validate the capabilities on each access authorization. A system employing access control lists, on the other hand, requires higher overhead in searching the entire access control list associated with the object. An access control list could be very long and difficult to specify in a large and diverse distributed environment. Capability systems are more scalable since access verification is independent of the size of the system. Furthermore, for the purpose of *separation of policy and mechanism*, modern operating systems usually adopt a methodology that centralizes all access control policies in an authorization server and requires that all object servers be restricted to contain only basic mechanisms to enforce these policies. Distributed and local checking of capabilities at an object server is better adapted to such an environment, because otherwise, either an object server needs to request the authorization server for each access request (high communication overhead) or the authorization information needs to be distributed and possibly even duplicated to each object server (greater difficulty of managing authorization information). With these benefits, it can be easily understood that why most modern operating systems use capabilities for access control (to name a few: Eden[3], Accent[70], Mach[71], and Amoeba[80]). Therefore, management of capabilities in an efficient and secure way becomes one of the most important topics of contemporary distributed systems.

CHAPTER 3
EFFICIENT AUTHENTICATION WITH UNCERTIFIED KEYS

3.1 Motivation

The KSL protocol for repeated authentication mentioned earlier requires five messages for its initial authentication and three messages for each subsequent authentication session. Later, Neuman and Stubblebine presented another nonce-based protocol which requires only four messages for the initial authentication but still three messages for each subsequent authentication. However, the Neuman-Stubblebine protocol offers apparently improved protocol efficiency by sacrificing the security of the protocol, in that a weaker set of formalized goals [13] is achieved than that achieved by the KSL protocol. More specifically, the Neuman-Stubblebine protocol lacks the final belief reached by the KSL protocol: principal A is convinced that its communicating peer, principal B, also trusts the session key to be used between them [65, 79]. This is mainly because of the nature of the Neuman-Stubblebine protocol, in which A has never received any message encrypted with the session key, either directly or indirectly via the authentication server, from B. That is, a full nonce handshaking between two principals to demonstrate mutual trusts on the session key to each other is not actually performed in the Neuman-Stubblebine protocol.

22

Syverson [79] detailed the discussion of the discrepancy between these two protocols and demonstrated how the Neuman-Stubblebine protocol could be attacked and what implementation assumptions need to be made to prevent against those kinds of attacks. An interesting question inspired by Syverson's discussion is whether there exists any protocol which can achieve the same formalized goals as the KSL protocol but is no more expensive, in terms of the number of messages, than the Neuman-Stubblebine protocol. The objective of this chapter is to provide a positive answer to this question with a new nonce-based authentication protocol using *uncertified keys*.

Most existing authentication protocols in distributed systems achieve identification and key distributions on the belief that the use of a uncertified key, i.e. a key whose freshness and authenticity cannot be verified immediately by its receiving principal while being received, should be avoided in the course of an authentication process. However, we claim that using a uncertified key prudently can give performance advantages and not necessarily reduce the security of authentication protocols, so long as the validity of the key can be verified at the end of an authentication process [41]. The new proposed protocol using uncertified keys can achieve both the lower message overhead of the Neuman-Stubblebine protocol and the stronger authentication goals of the KSL protocol. In fact, its total number of messages is shown to be minimal of all authentication protocols with the same formalized goals of authentication. In the following, the properties which make the protocol optimal in terms of message complexity are elaborated, and a formal logical analysis of the protocol is performed. The proposed protocol is extended further to prevent the *session key compromise* problem and to support repeated authentication in a symmetric and flexible way, without losing its optimality. Finally, the protocol is generalized to a version applicable for *inter-domain* authentication and key distribution.

3.2   The Proposed Nonce-based Protocol

The assumptions of the environment where the protocol is to be operated and of possible attacks are basically the same as those assumed by most existing authentication protocols. Two principals, A and B, desire to authenticate each other and to obtain a shared session key for subsequent communication. A trusted authentication server S shares a master key with each principal and is capable of producing good session keys and sending them securely on the requests of principals. No clock synchronization among machines is assumed, so nonce-based challenge/response exchanges are used to guarantee the freshness of messages.

The message flow of the protocol is shown in Figure 1 and the contents of each message is as follows:

Message 1 $A \rightarrow S :$ A, B, N_a

Message 2 $S \rightarrow B :$ $\{A, B, N_a, K_{ab}\}_{K_{as}}, \{A, B, N_a, K_{ab}\}_{K_{bs}}$

Message 3 $B \rightarrow A :$ $\{A, B, N_a, K_{ab}\}_{K_{as}}, \{N_a\}_{K_{ab}}, N_b$

Message 4 $A \rightarrow B :$ $\{N_b\}_{K_{ab}}$

Principal A initiates the authentication by sending S a plaintext message containing

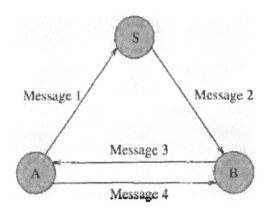

Figure 3.1. A nonce-based authentication protocol

the identities of itself and the desired communicating peer B, and a nonce N_a (message 1). After S receives this message, it generates a session key K_{ab} and appends it to the identities of both parties and nonce N_a to form two credentials, one for A and the other for B. Both credentials have exactly the same contents, but one is encrypted with A's master key K_{as}, and the other is encrypted with B's master key K_{bs}. S sends both credentials to B (message 2), who then decrypts the second one and finds out that A wants to authenticate with B mutually, that N_a is the nonce issued by A, and that K_{ab} is generated by S to be used as a session key for future communication between A and B. B then forwards the first credential from S to A, and also sends an encrypted N_a with K_{ab} and another nonce N_b (message 3). Upon receiving them, A decrypts the credential to get K_{ab} and verifies its freshness by checking the presence of N_a. A also authenticates B by decrypting the encrypted part with K_{ab} and comparing the result with N_a. If they match, A encrypts N_b with K_{ab} and sends it back to B (massage 4) to prove its identity to B.

3.2.1 Informal Analysis

In the protocol, A verifies the identity of B by checking whether the peer principal is able to encrypt nonce N_a with session key K_{ab}. This verification is based upon two beliefs of A. The first one is that on the request of authentication (message 1), S will issue a credential containing N_a and K_{ab} and encrypted with K_{bs} for principal B (message 2). The second belief of A is that only S and B share master key K_{bs}, so no other principal except B is able to send the encrypted N_a with K_{ab} (message 3). Therefore, the protocol prevents against impersonation of B by the assumptions of the correct behavior of the authentication server and of the secrecy of master keys. Furthermore, since nonce N_a is used only for the current session, replay of old messages issued by either S or B will be detected.

On the other side, B verifies the identity of A by the use of uncertified session keys. When B receives message 2, B has no way to tell whether the message is either a replay or an impersonation attempt initiated by a malicious principal C. B only presumes that some principal who claims to be A wants to authenticate each other with itself *for the current session*. To verify message 2 is authentic and fresh, B needs to use (and temporarily believe) the uncertified session key K_{ab} to encrypt N_a and also sends its own nonce N_b in the clear. If A returns message 4 as expected, B believes in the authenticity and freshness of K_{ab}. If message 2 is only a replay (either copy-and-replay or suppress-and-play), A will detect it and thus will not respond with a normal message 4 (instead, A probably sends back an error message to inform B that a replay is possibly occurring), so B knows K_{ab} is not fresh. If principal C wants to impersonate A and initiates an authentication process, it is incapable of producing message 4 since K_{ab} is intelligible to C. Therefore, B can verify its temporal belief as to the authenticity and freshness of message 2 by a nonce challenge/response exchange with A. Note that B authenticates A based upon the beliefs similar to those on which A bases to authenticate B.

3.3   A Formal Protocol Analysis Using BAN Logic

We now analyze the proposed protocol with BAN Logic. To describe the protocol formally, each message of the protocol is converted to an idealized form recommended by BAN Logic:

$$\text{Message 2}\quad S \rightarrow B: \quad \{N_a, A \overset{K_{ab}}{\leftrightarrow} B\}_{K_{as}}, \{N_a, A \overset{K_{ab}}{\leftrightarrow} B\}_{K_{bs}}$$

$$\text{Message 3}\quad B \rightarrow A: \quad \{N_a, A \overset{K_{ab}}{\leftrightarrow} B\}_{K_{as}}, \{N_a, A \overset{K_{ab}}{\leftrightarrow} B\}_{K_{ab}}$$

$$\text{Message 4}\quad A \rightarrow B: \quad \{N_b, A \overset{K_{ab}}{\leftrightarrow} B\}_{K_{ab}}$$

The first message is omitted since it is in the clear and thus provides no guarantee about the properties of the protocol. The result is as if S acted spontaneously. Message 2 expresses the fact that both credentials from S contain nonce N_a and session key K_{ab} to be shared between A and B (which is represented by $A \overset{K_{ab}}{\leftrightarrow} B$). The first component of message 3 indicates that B faithfully forwards the first component of message 2 to A, and the second component means that B temporarily trusts K_{ab}, and uses it to encrypt N_a to imply to A that it would like to share K_{ab} with A upon subsequent verification. The last message indicates that A has verified the freshness of K_{ab}, and responds to B's challenge by encrypting N_b with K_{ab}.

The initial assumptions of the protocol in BAN Logic notation are:

Key $\quad$ 1. $A \models A \overset{K_{as}}{\leftrightarrow} S$

$\qquad\quad$ 2. $B \models B \overset{K_{bs}}{\leftrightarrow} S$

$\qquad\quad$ 3. $S \models A \overset{K_{as}}{\leftrightarrow} S$

$\qquad\quad$ 4. $S \models B \overset{K_{bs}}{\leftrightarrow} S$

$\qquad\quad$ 5. $S \models A \overset{K_{ab}}{\leftrightarrow} B$

Server $\quad$ 1. $A \models (S \Mapsto A \overset{K}{\leftrightarrow} B)$

$\qquad\quad$ 2. $B \models (S \Mapsto A \overset{K}{\leftrightarrow} B)$

Freshness $\quad$ 1. $A \models \sharp(N_a)$

$\qquad\qquad$ 2. $B \models \sharp(N_b)$

$\qquad\qquad$ 3. $B \models \sharp(A \overset{K}{\leftrightarrow} B)$

The first four assumptions in the *Key* group specify the initial beliefs (the symbol $\models$ stands for "believes") about the secrecy of master keys between the principals and the authentication server. The fifth denotes that session key K_{ab} can only be generated by S. The next group (*Server*) indicates the trusts that A and B have on the server to generate a good session key (the symbol $\Mapsto$ means "has jurisdiction over"). The last group of assumptions is about the freshness (represented by the symbol $\sharp$) of nonces and keys. The first two indicate that each principal can issue a nonce and trusts only the nonce issued by that principal. The last one is needed by

B for attempting to use a uncertified key. As pointed out in the BAN Logic paper about the Needham-Schroeder protocol [13], the last assumption is not as obvious as others initially, but can be verified later by the protocol itself.

The formal proof of the protocol using the postulates of BAN Logic is presented as follow. First, A sends S a cleartext message containing a nonce. S then sends message 2 to B, that is:

$$B \triangleleft \{N_a, A \overset{K_{ab}}{\leftrightarrow} B\}_{K_{as}}, \{N_a, A \overset{K_{ab}}{\leftrightarrow} B\}_{K_{bs}},$$

where $\triangleleft$ means "sees". B can decrypt the second component of this message with K_{bs}. Applying the message-meaning rule to it, we can deduce:

$$B \models S \hspace{-0.3em}\sim (A \overset{K_{ab}}{\leftrightarrow} B),$$

where $\hspace{-0.3em}\sim$ means "once said". With the application of the nonce-verification rule to the above assertion and the assumption $B \models \sharp(A \overset{K}{\leftrightarrow} B)$, we obtain:

$$B \models S \models A \overset{K_{ab}}{\leftrightarrow} B$$

With the jurisdiction rule, we immediately get:

$$B \models A \overset{K_{ab}}{\leftrightarrow} B$$

B, temporarily trusting K_{ab}, generates message 3 and sends it to A, thus:

$$A \triangleleft \{N_a, A \overset{K_{ab}}{\leftrightarrow} B\}_{K_{as}}, \{N_a, A \overset{K_{ab}}{\leftrightarrow} B\}_{K_{ab}}$$

A can decrypt the first component encrypted with K_{as}. Since S knows N_a to be fresh, we can apply the message-meaning rule, leading to:

$$A \models S \hspace{-0.3em}\sim (A \overset{K_{ab}}{\leftrightarrow} B)$$

Applying the nonce-verification and jurisdiction rules in a way similar to the above described, we obtain:

$$A \models A \overset{K_{ab}}{\leftrightarrow} B$$

After getting K_{ab}, A uses it to decrypt the second component of message 3 and checks the presence of N_a. Therefore, the message-meaning rule applies:

$$A \models B \mid\!\sim (A \overset{K_{ab}}{\leftrightarrow} B)$$

With the nonce-jurisdiction rule, we can obtain:

$$A \models B \models A \overset{K_{ab}}{\leftrightarrow} B$$

Then A replies B with message 4. B deduces from the message that A believes in the session key. With an analysis similar to the one applied to the second component of message 3, we can get:

$$B \models A \models A \overset{K_{ab}}{\leftrightarrow} B$$

In conclusion, the final beliefs of both principals achieved by this protocol are:

$$A \models A \overset{K_{ab}}{\leftrightarrow} B \qquad\qquad B \models A \overset{K_{ab}}{\leftrightarrow} B$$

$$A \models B \models A \overset{K_{ab}}{\leftrightarrow} B \qquad B \models A \models A \overset{K_{ab}}{\leftrightarrow} B$$

which are exactly the formalized goals of authentication for all authentication protocols as recommended by the authors of BAN Logic. It should be noticed that these goals can be achieved with only four messages.

3.4 Countering Session Key Compromises

Like the original Needham-Schroeder protocol [62], the final beliefs of our protocol are reached assuming that B accepts the session key as new upon receiving it, though the assumption can be verified as the protocol proceeds. Not surprisingly, our protocol is also vulnerable to the session key compromise attack as pointed out by

Denning and Sacco [21] in regard to the original Needham-Schroeder protocol. That is, if an intruder C compromised an old session key and copied messages 2 and 4 of the protocol run in which the session key was used, C can pretend to B as it were A. B is incapable, by the protocol itself, of knowing whether a session key has been compromised or not. Note that message 4 of the protocol only verifies to B whether the session key is a replay or the result of an impersonation attempt, *if the key is not compromised.*

This possible attack can be prevented by including timestamps in messages as suggested by Denning and Sacco [21], a suggestion which requires clock synchronization of all the machines, however. Alternatively, the solution proposed by Needham and Schroeder [63] for their original protocol requires B to generate its own nonce initially and S to include this nonce in the message containing the session key. This unfortunately leads to at least two more messages in a protocol run. The following text describes an enhancement of our proposed protocol to counter this impersonation attack, requiring neither time synchronization nor additional messages.

Without taking consideration of the robustness of cryptographic algorithms and the possibility of brute-force cryptanalysis, session keys are easier to compromise than master keys because of operational reasons. Session keys are used over a relatively longer time period and are usually stored in (probably insecure) local memory or registers for efficient encryption and decryption for the entire communication session. In general, attacks on session keys can be prevented effectively by raising the quality of session keys (e.g. using longer keys) or improving the protocol itself to reduce the vulnerability resulting from insecure local memory and communication links. The strategy we take is to have S issue another key K_t, along with K_{ab}, to the principals in the protocol. K_t is used just for the current authentication session and is discarded immediately after authentication. The improved protocol becomes:

Message 1 $\quad A \to S: \quad A, B, N_a$

Message 2 $\quad S \to B: \quad \{A, B, N_a, K_{ab}, K_t\}_{K_{as}}, \{A, B, N_a, K_{ab}, K_t\}_{K_{bs}}$

Message 3 $\quad B \to A: \quad \{A, B, N_a, K_{ab}, K_t\}_{K_{as}}, \{N_a, K_{ab}\}_{K_t}, N_b$

Message 4 $\quad A \to B: \quad \{N_b, K_{ab}\}_{K_t}$

K_t is issued by S and included in both credentials of message 2. It is used by B to encrypt N_a and K_{ab} to tell A that B temporarily trusts both keys K_{ab} and K_t. A verifies B's temporal trusts on these keys by checking the presence of N_a within the first credential in message 3, and sends back to B the encrypted N_b and K_{ab} with key K_t. After K_t is used by A for encrypting message 4, it is removed right away from the local memory of A's machine. After message 4 is received and verified, B also immediately removes K_t from its local memory.

The use of K_t is exclusively for authentication only. A new K_t is generated by the authentication server S for each initial mutual authentication. An intruder may have compromised K_{ab} and may replay old authentication messages, but will fail to impersonate A in a run of this improved protocol, since the intruder is unable to encrypt message 4 with the new K_t. K_t is much more difficult to break than K_{ab} because it is used by (and meaningful to) A and B only for a very brief period.

Another advantage of this improved protocol is that the same K_{ab} can be used for multiple sessions, since each session initiation is checked by a different K_t.

3.5 Repeated Authentication

Heavily utilized authentication servers may become a performance and security bottleneck in the system. If a system operates in a relatively benign environment and the session keys distributed possess pretty good quality, it is possible to reduce the workload of authentication servers and the corresponding communication overhead by repeating the use of a previous session key for subsequent authentication sessions. Protocols for repeated authentication usually distribute some credentials (which are often called *tickets* and will be referred to as *session-key certificates* in this paper) to principals during an initial authentication session. In a subsequent authentication session, a session-key certificate is used to convey securely a session key distributed earlier to the principal who can recognize that certificate, without the need to contact the authentication server again. In the following section, we show how our protocol can be extended to deal with repeated authentication, in a more secure and symmetrical way than the KSL and Neuman-Stubblebine protocols.

3.5.1 Initial Authentication: Getting Session-key Certificates

Messages 3 and 4 in the initial authentication protocol are extended further to include session-key certificates for repeated authentication.

Message 1 $\quad A \to S : \quad A, B, N_a$

Message 2 $\quad S \to B : \quad \{A, B, N_a, K_{ab}, K_t\}_{K_{as}}, \{A, B, N_a, K_{ab}, K_t\}_{K_{bs}}$

Message 3 $\quad B \to A : \quad \{A, B, N_a, K_{ab}, K_t\}_{K_{as}}, \{N_a, K_{ab}\}_{K_t}, N_b, \{A, B, T_b, K_{ab}\}_{K_{bs}}$

Message 4 $\quad A \to B : \quad \{N_b, K_{ab}\}_{K_t},$

$$\{A, B, T_a, K_{ab}\}_{K_{as}}$$

In message 3, B also sends A a session-key certificate which contains the identities of both A and B, session key K_{ab}, and a generalized timestamp T_b, suggested by the KSL protocol. It is encrypted with the master key of B. After checking the validity of message 3, A also returns B with a session-key certificate which contains similar information but is encrypted with A's own master key. Since a session-key certificate is encrypted with the master key of its issuer, it is only recognizable to the issuer. The purpose of a generalized timestamp is to limit the validity of a certificate, corresponding to the *local time* of the issuer. Therefore, the assumption of global clock synchronization is not required by using timestamps this way.

3.5.2 Subsequent Authentication: Exchanging the Certificates

After the initial authentication, A and B hold session-key certificates for each other. When the communication session between A and B following the initial authentication is completed, K_{ab} is removed from the local memory of both principals' machines. Since the session key does not need to be kept in the memory of principal

A's machine after an initial communication session as in the KSL and Neuman-Stubblebine protocols, this method of protecting session keys is more secure than those protocols. It also distributes the risk of compromising all the session keys of A at the same time if A is communicating with multiple peer principals, since each session-key certificate of A is held by a distinct principal. When A wants to repeat an authentication with B next time, A initiates a protocol as follows:

Message 1' $A \rightarrow B$: $\{A, B, T_b, K_{ab}\}_{K_{bs}}, N'_a$

Message 2' $B \rightarrow A$: $\{A, B, T_a, K_{ab}\}_{K_{as}}, \{N'_a\}_{K_{ab}}, N'_b$

Message 3' $A \rightarrow B$: $\{N'_b, N'_a\}_{K_{ab}}$

A sends the session-key certificate previously issued by B and nonce N'_a in message 1'. After verifying that the certificate is still fresh, B temporarily trusts session key K_{ab} and uses it to encrypt N'_a. B then sends back the matching session-key certificate issued earlier by A, the encrypted N'_a, and a new nonce N'_b (message 2'). The last message shows that A has already trusted K_{ab} and verified the identity of B. Upon receiving it, B verifies its trust on K_{ab} and the identity of A.

The subsequent authentication protocol is actually similar in both spirit and style to the initial authentication protocol. The difference between them is that in the former two principals exchanges session-key certificates originally generated by each other, and in the latter A initiates S to generate a session key for both principals and requires B to forward the session key to itself. It should be noticed that possession of a session-key certificate only means holding some key information for another principal. It does not provide any authentication guarantee. The capability of recognizing (decrypting) the certificate and then encrypting a nonce with the session key is still needed to verify the identity of a principal. Note also that even in the initial authentication protocol B sends a session-key certificate to A (message 3) prior to verifying the session key, B will not accept the session-key certificate from A as valid if the nonce response from A is different from the one expected.

In addition to protecting the session keys more securely, another advantage of our repeated authentication protocol over the KSL and Neuman-Stubblebine protocols is that either A or B can initiate a subsequent authentication. The subsequent authentication protocol initiated by B is symmetrical to the one shown above. Both the KSL and Neuman-Stubblebine protocols presume the role of A as a client and the role of B as a server in an initial authentication. Their roles do not change during subsequent authentications. However, our protocol does not assume the role of any principal, rendering more flexibility as to who can initiate a subsequent authentication. In modern client-server type distributed systems, principal B, being a server of client A in the current communication session, could be a client of A as a server in the next session. For these reasons, our authentication protocol is better adapted to another distributed system paradigm, the peer-to-peer communication style.

3.5.3 Prevention of Oracle Session Attacks

Encrypting N_a' in the last message of a repeated authentication provides an association between both message 2' and 3' in the same protocol run. Its main purpose is to prevent the oracle session attack [10], in which an intruder starts two separate authentication sessions with principals A and B such that it can utilize the messages in one session to impersonate a principal successfully in the other session.

Let us demonstrate an attack scenario with a version of our repeated authentication protocol without encrypting N'_a in message 3' (Figure 2):

(1) $C \rightarrow B$: $\{A, B, T_b, K_{ab}\}_{K_{b_s}}, N'_c$

(2) $B \rightarrow A$: $\{A, B, T_a, K_{ab}\}_{K_{a_s}}, \{N'_c\}_{K_{ab}}, N'_b$ —————— intercepted by C

(3) $C \rightarrow A$: $\{A, B, T_b, K_{ab}\}_{K_{a_s}}, N'_b$

(4) $A \rightarrow B$: $\{A, B, T_b, K_{ab}\}_{K_{b_s}}, \{N'_b\}_{K_{ab}}, N'_a$ —————— intercepted by C

(5) $C \rightarrow B$: $\{N'_b\}_{K_{ab}}$

An intruder C, who has copied a session-key certificate $\{A, B, T_b, K_{ab}\}_{K_{b_s}}$ during an initial authentication or an earlier repeated authentication session, pretends to be A by sending B that certificate and nonce N'_c. B thinks that this authentication request was from A and responds with A's session-key certificate $\{A, B, T_a, K_{ab}\}_{K_{a_s}}$, nonce response $\{N'_a\}_{K_{ab}}$, and a new nonce N'_b. All are intercepted by C. Then C pretends to be B by sending A (the oracle) the certificate and nonce N'_b that it just obtained from B. A also thinks that this authentication request was from B and responds with B's session-key certificate $\{A, B, T_b, K_{ab}\}_{K_{b_s}}$, nonce response $\{N'_b\}_{K_{ab}}$, and a new nonce N'_a. This message again is intercepted by C. C thus can impersonate A successfully by just passing the nonce response $\{N'_b\}_{K_{ab}}$ to B. Although K_{ab} is not compromised,

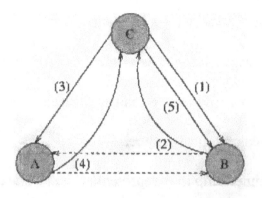

Figure 3.2. An oracle session attack by an intruder C

A's privileges still could be abused by C by just replaying some encrypted messages (also encrypted with K_{ab} intercepted in an earlier communication session).

This type of attack can succeed if there is no explicit association between messages 2' and 3'. With N'_a encrypted in both messages, it is ensured that message 3' obtained by B belongs to the same protocol run as message 2' it has sent. This technique is a realization of the suggestion by some authentication protocol researchers [2, 23] that *messages in a particular protocol run should be logically linked in a manner such that the re-use of messages from a previous run or the introduction of messages from a concurrent run can be detected.*

3.5.4 Timestamp and Logical Analysis

In distinction from the initial authentication protocol, a principal running the protocol for subsequent authentication checks the freshness of a session key by using the generalized timestamp associated with it. However, even with a generalized timestamp, a principal still cannot tell whether or not the sending of a session-key certificate by the peer principal is a replay or an impersonation attempt, if the lifetime of the certificate has not ended yet. Using generalized timestamps this way actually does not guarantee message freshness as effectively as provided by nonce challenges. A principal still needs to verify that an authentication message is fresh by a nonce handshaking with the communicating peer.

The generalized timestamp that represents the lifetime of a session-key is solely determined by the issuer of the certificate. This autonomy may result in a pair of related certificates with very different lifetimes. This timestamp discrepancy problem can be solved easily by including some timestamp information in the second component (encrypted with K_t) of message 3 in the initial authentication protocol. When the receiver principal obtains this information, that receiver can refer to it for determining the timestamp parameters of the session-key certificate to be issued in message 4. Because no full negotiation between both principals about the timestamps is performed (actually not a necessity) and it is meaningless for a principal to issue a certificate which lives longer than that issued by the peer principal, this way tends to make the certificate issued by the principal sending message 4 expire earlier.

The repeated authentication protocol can be analyzed by using BAN Logic in a way very similar to the analysis for the initial authentication protocol, and the four formalized goals of authentication can also be achieved.

3.6   Inter-domain Authentication and Key Distribution

The authentication protocol we have proposed is an intra-domain protocol, in that there exists a centralized authentication server trusted by all principals in one administrative domain. However, inter-domain authentication is required by many network applications which need communications across administrative domains [25, 26, 69]. It is reasonable to assume that all the domains and the trust relationships among them form a hierarchical tree structure, just like the real world management structure, and the master key of each principal is confidential only to the principal itself and the authentication server in the domain to which the principal belongs. Any authentication request message from a principal A to another principal B in a different domain needs to go up from A along the domain structure tree to their common ancestor node and then go down to B. Inter-domain authentication deserves more careful thought because of the emerging popularity of many inter-network applications such as electronic commerce on *World Wide Web* . Prior to extending the protocol to deal with inter-domain authentication, some important design principles which differentiate inter-domain authentication from intra-domain authentication are listed below.

- The message complexity and encryption overhead should be reduced as much as possible because more system facilities (multiple authentication servers and gateways) are involved in an inter-domain authentication.

- Because of the hierarchical characteristic of the domain structure, the workload of an authentication server at a higher level in the hierarchy will be greater since each pair of principals in different sub-domains need its service directly or indirectly to achieve authentication and key distribution. To reduce the possibility that a high-level authentication server becomes a performance bottleneck, repeated authentication should be used whenever possible.

- The use of timestamps, although effective in reducing the message complexity, should be avoided in an inter-domain authentication, since the assumption of proper clock synchronization among multiple machines is much more difficult to guarantee if the machines reside in different administrative domains.

- Inter-domain authentication should be transparent to local principals. That is, the mechanisms designed for inter-domain authentication should not interfere with the original intra-domain authentication mechanisms at local machines. If this transparency property can be maintained, any addition or modification of features for inter-domain authentication has an impact only upon authentication servers. Because the modules for intra-domain authentication at local machines are not affected, original security properties of the intra-domain protocol could be preserved.

3.6.1 Protocol Extension

The proposed protocol can be extended naturally to an version for inter-domain authentication. For simplicity, we only describe how the protocol is extended to a two-level one here. An extension of the protocol to a general multi-level version can be designed similarly. In the following, it is assumed that principal A and principal B belong to Domain 1 and Domain 2, respectively. S_1 is the authentication server in Domain 1 and S_2 in Domain 2. S_H is a high-level authentication server which is trusted by and share a master key with either S_1 or S_2.

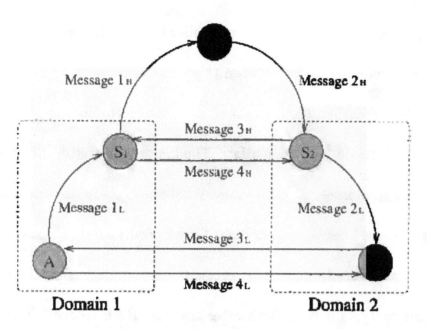

Figure 3.3. Two-level inter-domain authentication

Message 1_L $A \rightarrow S_1$: A, B, N_a

Message 1_H $S_1 \rightarrow S_H$: S_1, S_2, N_1

Message 2_H $S_H \rightarrow S_2$: $\{S_1, S_2, N_1, K_{12}, K_{th}\}_{K_{1h}}, \{S_1, S_2, N_1, K_{12}, K_{th}\}_{K_{2h}}$

Message 3_H $S_2 \rightarrow S_1$: $\{S_1, S_2, N_1, K_{12}, K_{th}\}_{K_{1h}}, \{N_1, K_{12}\}_{K_{th}}, N_2$

Message 4_H $S_1 \rightarrow S_2$: $\{N_2, K_{12}\}_{K_{1h}}, \{A, B, N_a, K_{ab}, K_{tl}\}_{K_{a1}}, \{A, B, N_a, K_{ab}, K_{tl}\}_{K_{1t}}$

Message 2_L $S_2 \rightarrow B$: $\{A, B, N_a, K_{ab}, K_{tl}\}_{K_{a1}}, \{A, B, N_a, K_{ab}, K_{tl}\}_{K_{b2}}$

Message 3_L $B \rightarrow A$: $\{A, B, N_a, K_{ab}, K_{tl}\}_{K_{a1}}, \{N_a, K_{ab}\}_{K_{tl}}, N_b$

Message 4_L $A \rightarrow B$: $\{N_b, K_{ab}\}_{K_{tl}}$

The protocol consists of two levels, one for the authentication between S_1 and S_2 (messages 1_H to 4_H) and the other for the authentication between A and B (messages 1_L to 4_L). After S_1 receives the authentication request from A, it checks if B is in its own domain. If not, S_1 initiates an authentication process with S_2, via their commonly trusted server S_H, in a way similar to the intra-domain authentication protocol. The main difference between this server-level authentication and the original principal-level authentication is that in message 4_H, S_1 not only responds S_2's challenge but also sends two credentials. The first one is destined to A and thus encrypted with A's master key K_{a1}, and the second one is for B but encrypted with the session key K_{12}, used between S_1 and S_2, S_2 then decrypts the second credential after receiving it, and gets to know that credential is for a principal B in its own domain, and thus encrypts it with B's master key K_{b2}. Both credentials are sent to B, and A and B execute the protocol just like the intra-domain authentication case.

We would like to contrast this extended protocol with the design principles listed earlier. Since one extra message must be required for forwarding the authentication request from S_1 to S_2 no matter what authentication protocol is used, actually only three more messages are needed to achieve an authentication between two principals in different domains. If the session key used between authentication servers has good quality, and many pairs of principals in their domains want to authenticate mutually during a relatively short period, only one server-level authentication process needs to be performed for the first pair of principals. Therefore, the overhead caused by the inter-domain authentication can be amortized among many sessions. With this strategy, the server-authentication part of the protocol can be further enhanced such that S_1 and S_2 exchange some information to determine when they need to run a full handshaked authentication next time. Because timestamps are not used at all in an inter-domain authentication, synchronization of machine clocks is still not

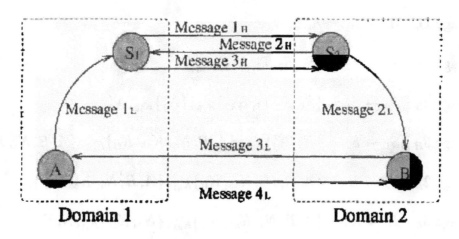

Figure 3.4. Repeated inter-domain authentication

needed. Moreover, the protocol is absolutely transparent to local principals since A and B do not even know a server-level authentication has ever been activated for their authentication session. So any modification to the inter-domain authentication mechanisms at authentication servers will not have an effect on the authentication software within local machines.

3.6.2 Using Repeated Authentication

As we have argued, repeated authentication should be used whenever possible for inter-domain authentication, to reduce the computation workload and communication overhead of high level servers. If we assume S_1 and S_2 have obtained each other's session-key certificates (It is not included in the extended protocol above, but can be accommodated easily.) during their initial authentication, they can run a repeated authentication protocol when any pair of principals in two domains (not necessarily A and B) want to authenticate mutually next time, as follows.

Message 1_L $A \rightarrow S_1:$ A, B, N_a

Message 1_H $S_1 \rightarrow S_2:$ $\{S_1, S_2, T_2, K_{12}\}_{K_{2h}}, N_1'$

Message 2_H $S_2 \rightarrow S_1:$ $\{S_1, S_2, T_1, K_{12}\}_{K_{1h}}, \{N_1'\}_{K_{12}}, N_2'$

Message 3_H $S_1 \rightarrow S_2:$ $\{N_1', N_2'\}_{K_{12}}, \{A, B, N_a, K_{ab}, K_{tl}\}_{K_{a1}}, \{A, B, N_a, K_{ab}, K_{tl}\}_{K_{12}}$

Message 2_L $S_2 \rightarrow B:$ $\{A, B, N_a, K_{ab}, K_{tl}\}_{K_{a1}}, \{A, B, N_a, K_{ab}, K_{tl}\}_{K_{b2}}$

Message 3_L $B \rightarrow A:$ $\{A, B, N_a, K_{ab}, K_{tl}\}_{K_{a1}}, \{N_a, K_{ab}\}_{K_{tl}}, N_b$

Message 4_L $A \rightarrow B:$ $\{N_b, K_{ab}\}_{K_{tl}}$

Again, the message which needs to be taken special care of is message 3_H, in which the second credential must be decrypted with K_{12} and then encrypted with S_{b2} before being sent to principal B. Using repeated authentication this way results in only two extra messages in one authentication session. In fact, these extra messages can even be saved if the level of using repeated authentication is lowered to the authentication between A and B. That is, both principals exchange their session-key certificates during an initial authentication which must go through the authentication servers, and run an repeated authentication between themselves without bothering the servers again. In summary, repeated authentication can be switched on and off autonomously at any level, depending upon the security environment and the quality of session keys.

CHAPTER 4
MODELING OF COMPLEX SECURITY POLICIES

4.1 Motivation

As mentioned in Chapter 2, many computer applications in the business and commercial world need complex security policies which are difficult to enforce by using a mandatory multilevel security model because their enforcement must violate the basic properties of the mathematical structure upon which the model is based. Nor can these policies be modeled by a discretionary security model like the HRU access control matrix since the access characteristics of these applications demand some degree of mandatory control. Moreover, different types of complex security requirements may exist in an organization at the same time. To incorporate these security requirements, security administrators are often forced to resort to less graceful and complicated methods to satisfy each requirement individually. Thus, the difficulty of maintaining a secure computing environment satisfying all specific security requirements is increased considerably. Therefore, there is a definite need for a uniform and powerful security model to enforce all these complex security policies for which both mandatory multilevel security and discretionary access control are inadequate.

An effective access control model based on boolean expressions of classified categories is proposed and implemented for this purpose [43]. In the following sections, we first systematically categorize *multilevel exceptions*, and show many security policies required by commercial applications are actually examples of these multilevel exceptions. The model is described first in an informal way and then defined formally. The power of this model is demonstrated by its capability of expressing a rich set of access patterns from subjects to objects elegantly and uniformly. We also prove that all security policies which can be enforced by a conventional multilevel security model is only a subset of all the security policies that can be enforced by this new model. Furthermore, it is elaborated how this model can be employed to enforce all multilevel exceptions and other complex security policies. Finally, a distributed implementation of the model on a client/server architecture with remote procedure call as the communication mechanism is described.

4.2   Categorization of Multilevel Exceptions

Since a multilevel security model is built on a lattice of security classes, *information flow* (as a result of a read or write operation from a subject to an object) can occur between two different classes according to the direction as permitted by the dominance relation used to construct the lattice [19, 20, 45]. In other words, information can flow from a class A to another class B only if A dominates or is dominated by B, as regulated by the access control rule of the model. Information cannot flow between A and B if there exists no domination relation between two classes. *Multilevel exceptions* are the information flows which violate the properties implied by the domination relation of a lattice. Unfortunately, many commercial applications can be found to require these multilevel exceptions, as elaborated as follows.

4.2.1 Multilevel Information Flow Exceptions

Information flow in a lattice-based model is transitive, i.e., if information is allowed to flow from class A to class B (which means either a subject in class A can write information into an object in class B or a subject in class B can read information from an object in class A), and from B to class C, then it is allowed to flow from A to C directly. However, some applications do exist where this transitive property is not desired. If the symbol "$\rightarrow$" is defined to represent the allowable direction of information flow between a pair of security classes and "$\nrightarrow$" to represent the prohibited direction of flow, then *transitivity exception* is formalized as $A \rightarrow B$ and $B \rightarrow C$, but $A \nrightarrow C$.

Another exception of multilevel information flow which is also often desired by some applications is *aggregation exception* [56, 57]. In a lattice-based model, if $A \rightarrow C$ and $B \rightarrow C$, then the aggregate of information from A and B, represented by $A \cup B$, should be allowed to flow to C. An aggregation exception is a violation of this property, which is formalized as $A \rightarrow C$ and $B \rightarrow C$, but $A \cup B \nrightarrow C$. In practice, this exception can be interpreted as after C sinks information from either A of B, it can not sink any information from the other class.

The dual problem of aggregation exception is *separation exception*. The most notable application is separation of duty, one of the most important ingredients in security policies and models concerning data integrity [6, 15, 46, 60, 72]. It specifies that information cannot flow from a single class, either A or B, to another class C, but only the aggregate of information from A and B, represented by $A \cup B$ can. This can be interpreted more practically as once information transfers from either A or B to C, the other must also transfer information to C. The information flowed to C from the first entity will not be valid or meaningful until information flow from the second entity happens. This requirement cannot be satisfied by a lattice-based model alone, and is formalized as $A \cup B \rightarrow C$, but $A \nrightarrow C$ and $B \nrightarrow C$.

It should be noticed that these exceptions are not direct violations of the dominance relation used to construct the lattice. Instead, they place more constraints on the flow of information among different classes than permitted by a lattice-based multilevel model.

4.2.2   Refining the Exceptions in Access Control

Although the three exceptions described above originate from the view point of information flow, they can be defined in terms of access control. In access control, the most basic operations for information transfer between entities are "read" and "write" (because other more abstract operations can be decomposed into these two basic operations). So $A \rightarrow B$ means subject A writes information to object B or subject B reads information from object A. Furthermore, when an access control model is defined, usually the security goal of the model is explicitly specified as either data confidentiality or data integrity. Therefore the multilevel information flow exceptions can be classified in the scope of access control, according to how subjects and objects interact with each other and whether the security concern is confidentiality or integrity. A taxonomy of these classified multilevel exceptions with subjects and objects interacting with read and write operations is shown in Figure

	Transitivity Exception	Aggregation Exception	Separation Exception
Integrity (write)	[i]	[iii]	[v]
Confidentiality (read)	[ii]	[iv]	[vi]

Figure 4.1. A taxonomy of multilevel exceptions. The meanings of symbols: "R"— read, "W" — write, "⊕" — exclusive or, "*" — and.

4.1. The following discussion details each exception and justifies its significance with a frequently-used commercial security policy.

Transitivity exception can be described in access control as a relation among two subjects and two objects in two different ways. The first way, concerned with data integrity (Figure 3 [i]), is that subject S_1 can write object O_1, O_1 can be read by subject S_2, and S_2 can write object O_2, but S_1 cannot write O_2 directly. This actually simulates the concept of "well-formed transactions" in the Clark/Wilson commercial integrity policy [15]. The other way, which concerns data confidentiality (Figure 3 [ii]), is that O_1 can be read by S_1, S_1 can write O_2, and O_2 can be read by S_2, but O_1 cannot be read by S_2 directly. An example of this exception is the data formatting software problem mentioned earlier, that is, raw data (O_1) can not be read by a user (S_2) directly without being converted to a specific format (O_2) by a formatting process (S_1).

Aggregation exception can also be refined in terms of access control according to whether the security concern is data integrity or data confidentiality. If data integrity is the concern (Figure 3 [iii]), then either subject S_1 or subject S_2 can write object O_3 initially. However, after O_3 is written by S_1, it cannot be written by S_2 any more, and vice versa. Any application which requires an object to be written by only one subject, but not a specific one, falls into this category of exception. For example, in a paperless office environment, an electronic check can be prepared by either of two accountants, but after it is prepared, the other accountant is not allowed to access it, to prevent malicious modification. If data confidentiality is the concern (Figure 3 [iv]), then subject S_3 can read either object O_1 or object O_2, but S_3 can not read the aggregate of both objects. This can be interpreted as that after S_3 reads O_1, it can not read O_2 any more, and vice versa. The Chinese Wall security policy [12] introduced in chapter 2 provides a generalized example of this exception.

Since the original concern of separation exception is data integrity, many practical examples can be found in the literature discussing integrity policies and models [15, 46, 60, 72]. A simple one is that an employee composing a business document and the employee who approves the document to be released must be two different persons, in order to satisfy the principle of separation of duty. It is described (Figure 3 [v]) by a relation between two subjects S_1 and S_2 and an object O_3. After a subject (e.g., S_1) writes O_3, only the other (S_2) is allowed to write that object. If data confidentiality is the concern (Figure 3 [vi]), separation exception means that subject S_3 is allowed to read both objects O_1 and O_2 initially, but once after S_3 reads one of them (e.g., O_1), it is only allowed to read the other object (O_2). An example similar to the one mentioned in [28] is that after a user of a dial-up commercial database system has accessed one stage of database information subscribed, he may only access the service charge menu before he is allowed to access the next stage of database.

It should be pointed out that, to enforce aggregation and separation exceptions, the access privilege of a subject S to an object O will be affected either by the accesses of other subjects to O or by S's earlier accesses to other objects. It is implicit that for the security model to enforce these exceptions, it must incorporate the concept of state with subjects and objects such that access privileges of subjects to objects will vary in different states. In the following, a new model called $BEAC$ [43] is proposed to enforce these multilevel exceptions.

4.3   Boolean Expression based Access Control

An innovative access control model based on boolean expressions of classified categories is presented here. The basic idea of the model is first described in an informal (and more understandable) way, and its analogy with the lock-key concept is emphasized. Then the model is formalized mathematically.

4.3.1   The Basic Model

In this Boolean Expression based Access Control ($BEAC$) model, all the entities within a computing system are divided into subjects and objects, each of which has its own security attribute. The security attribute of a subject S is a set of categories, represented by $CAT(S) = \{c_1, c_2, \cdots\}$ where each c_i is a category, specifying the accessing characteristics of S. Unlike those in multilevel security models, the category sets all together used here do not constitute a lattice. A category c can be created and assigned to S whenever it is necessary, and its exact meaning and role in accessing an object completely depend on the security attribute of the object. The security attribute of an object O is an *Access Control Expression*, $ACE(O)$, which is a boolean expression composed of categories assembled by any operators allowed in boolean algebra ("$*$" means AND, "$+$" means OR, and a bar over a category, e.g. $\bar{c}$, means negation). When S tries to access O, the access is granted if $ACE(O)$ is evaluated to TRUE with $CAT(S)$. The evaluation process of $ACE(O)$ is described as follows: Any category in $ACE(O)$ has a default value of 0 initially. Then each category c in $ACE(O)$ is checked to see if it is also present in $CAT(S)$. The value of c in $ACE(O)$ will be converted to 1 if $c \in CAT(S)$. $ACE(O)$ is then evaluated using boolean algebra and the result can only be either TRUE or FALSE.

In the *BEAC* model, it is assumed that multiple access operations, not limited to read and write, can be defined on each object (depending upon the type of the object) and one ACE can be independently defined for each access mode. However, only a single CAT is associated with each subject. For simplicity, we will assume only one ACE with each object (thus one access mode only or one ACE applied to all access modes) from now on, unless stated otherwise.

For instance, if the CAT of a subject S_i is $\{a, b, c\}$ and ACE of an object O_j is $< a * \bar{c} >$, S_i is not allowed to access O_j since the category c in $CAT(S_i)$ makes $ACE(O_j)$ FALSE $(a * \bar{c} = 1 * \bar{1} = 1 * 0 = 0)$. However, S_i is allowed to access another object O_k whose ACE is $< b + d + e >$, since the existence of a single b in $ACT(S_i)$ makes $ACE(O_k)$ true. As another example, a subject S_1 which represents an employee in the Department of Defense could have a $CAT = \{North\_Korea, nuclear\_weapon\}$, which implies that S_1 has access to the objects categorized as $North\_Korea$, $nuclear\_weapon$, or both. Another subject S_2 which works for the Department of State may have a $CAT = \{North\_Korea, China\}$, which implies that the job responsibility of S_2 requires that the person has the access rights to the objects categorized as $North\_Korea$, $China$, or both. Now if an object O_1 representing a secret document file has an $ACE = < North\_Korea >$, then it can be accessed by both S_1 and S_2, because $North\_Korea$ exists in both category sets of S_1 and S_2. Another object whose $ACE = < \overline{nuclear\_weapon} >$ can be accessed by S_2 (because the default value of $nuclear\_weapon$ is 0) but cannot by S_1 (since the $nuclear\_weapon$ in S_2 makes $ACE(O_1)$ false).

The wildcard character, represented by symbol "\$", is also adopted by $BEAC$ to represent any possible category in an ACE, except those already present in the ACE. Note that for obvious reasons, "\$" can only appear in an ACE and not in a CAT. Utilizing the wildcard character prudently is very effective in achieving some desired access patterns precisely. For instance, an object whose $ACE = < a * b * \bar{\$} >$ can be accessed only by a subject whose CAT contains only a and b and nothing else (because any other category in the CAT will make value of $ become 1). Moreover, the value of the wildcat character is always determined after the value-substitutions of all other categories in an ACE.

$BEAC$ has a great similarity with the lock-key concept used in discretionary access control [20]. The lock-key concept is very intuitive in that a subject holding a key k_i which can be used to open a lock l_j can access the object "locked" by l_j. In the $BEAC$ model, each category in an CAT virtually corresponds to a key, so the CAT of a subject corresponds to a set of different keys. On the other hand, the ACE of an object for one access mode corresponds to a "lock combination". An $ACE = <a * b>$ represents a complex lock which can only be opened with presence of both keys a and b simultaneously. An $ACE = <a + b>$ represents a generalized lock which can be opened by either key a or key b. An $ACE = <\bar{a}>$ means a lock which remains open initially but the existence of key a in the CAT of a subject will lock it. More vividly, one ACE of an object represents a combination of locks on the door to the room where the object is located, and a subject must have all the necessary keys to open the door, in order to access the object in the access mode associated with that ACE.

4.3.2 Adding States by Classifying Categories

Motivated by the fact that access privileges of subjects to objects need to be restricted or expanded in order to enforce some complex security policies such as aggregation and separation exceptions, the security attributes of a subject and/or an object must be changed dynamically, as a result of access operations, yet in a controllable way. To facilitate this requirement, categories in the CAT of a subject are divided into two different classes. The first class is called *reusable category*, which permanently belongs to a subject once it is assigned to the subject, until a system security administrator explicitly removes it from the CAT of the subject through privileged commands. It is analogue to a reusable key which can be used by a subject to open a lock (an ACE) as many times as the subject would like to. The second class of categories is *one-time category*, which is dynamically assigned to a subject when the subject needs it. As its name implies, a one-time category can be used by a subject only once, and regardless whether it makes an ACE TRUE or FALSE, it is deleted from the CAT of the subject after its first use. (It can be imagined that a key is stuck on the door immediately after it is inserted into the lock hole, whether or not it can help to open the complex lock. A common mailbox in an apartment is one such example.) A category c is "used" only when a subject whose CAT contains c tries to access an object in a mode whose associated ACE also contains c. In other words, a one-time category will not be removed from the CAT of an accessing subject if it does not appear in the ACE associated with that access mode. To differentiate these two classes of categories, a hat put on a category in a CAT is used to indicate a one-time category, e.g., $\hat{c}$.

The other way of changing a subject's privilege to an object by $BEAC$ is to classify the categories composing the ACE of an object into two different classes. A *persistent category* is a category whose value remains 1 once it is converted to 1. Contrasting with the lock-key concept, a persistent category corresponds to a lock which remains open once it is opened. A *non-persistent category* (lock), on the other hand, needs to be value-substituted (opened) each time the ACE is evaluated. Similarly, a $\hat{c}$ in an ACE indicates that c is a persistent category.

It should be noticed that changing an object's security attribute has a greater effect than just changing a subject's security attribute, because the access privileges of all other related subjects will possibly be expanded or restricted. It should be used very carefully such that only the exact access control desired is achieved. To safeguard this, a more conservative approach is employed. It is assumed that whenever a new access control requirement is desired on an object, a new boolean expression is generated just for that requirement and is then ANDed with the original ACE (so the new generated boolean expression has no interference with the original ACE).

To enforce a state-dependent complex security policy, both classifications of security attributes mentioned above are often required, as demonstrated subsequently.

4.3.3 Formal Definition of $BEAC$

The $BEAC$ model described above is now formalized mathematically. The security attribute of any subject S is a category set C,

$$CAT(S) = C = \{c_1, c_2, \cdots, c_k\}$$

where each category c_i in C is either reusable or one-time. Thus,

$$C = C_r \cup C_o$$

where C_r is the set of all reusable categories and C_o is the set of all one-time categories. The security attribute of any object O for an access mode M is a boolean function of a category set B,

$$ACE(O)_M = BE(B) = BE(b_1, b_2, \cdots, b_m)$$

where BE represents a boolean function and each category b_i in B is is either persistent or non-persistent. Thus,

$$B = B_p \cup B_n$$

where B_p is the set of all persistent categories and B_n is the set of all non-persistent categories.

The access control rule of $BEAC$ is:

An access of subject S with $CAT(S) = C$ to object O with $ACE(O)_M = BE(B)$ in mode M is

granted, if $Eva(BE(B))_C = $ TRUE or

denied, if $Eva(BE(B))_C = $ FALSE

where $Eva(BE(B))_C$ means evaluating $BE(B)$ with the input that, for each $b_i \in B$,

$b_i = $ TRUE, if $b_i \in C$ or

$b_i = $ FALSE, otherwise.

The rule for updating the security attributes of a subject and an object, as a result of an access attempt, contains two parts:

After the access attempt of subject S with $CAT(S) = C$ to object O with $ACE(O)_M = BE(B)$ in mode M, all the one-time categories of $CAT(S)$ which have been used are removed. Specifically,

$$CAT(S) = C' = C - T$$

where $T = C_o \cap B$. At the same time, all the persistent categories in B will keep values of TRUE. That is,

$$ACE(O) = BE(B')$$

where B' contains all the elements b_i's of B with $b_i =$ TRUE if $b_i \in C \cap B_p$.

When a subject tries to access an object in $BEAC$, the access control rule is applied for the authorization decision. No matter what the authorization result is, the security attribute updating rule is then applied to the CAT of the subject and the ACE of the object. This series of operations (authorization $\rightarrow$ object access $\rightarrow$ attribute updating) should be implemented as an atomic operation without any interrupt permitted.

4.4 Some Discussion of the Modeling Power of $BEAC$

The modeling power of the $BEAC$ model is obvious. Firstly, both authoritative and prohibitive access control can be expressed at the same time by one mechanism. This is more straightforward than using the set containment relation among subject's and object's categories in conventional multilevel security models for access control enforcement. Secondly, in addition to the same benefits above, the AND and OR operators used in $BEAC$ also make the expression of access control more flexible and elegant. Boolean expressions are believed to represent more accurately many practical security requirements than multilevel security with levels and categories. In fact, we will show later that the $BEAC$ model can enforce any security policy which is enforced by the conventional multilevel security model. Finally, the wildcard category used to generalize access patterns sometimes or to restrict them at other times is as powerful as using the wildcard character "*" in the shell of UNIX. The desirability of prohibitive rights and wildcard in specifying access rights is debatable [17]. However, the flexibility these mechanisms provide is useful for some special purposes, as shown later.

It's now demonstrated that a rich set of *static* access control among subjects to an object can be provided by the use of boolean expressions. Suppose that in a system, there exist three subjects S_1, S_2, and S_3 with $\{a\}$, $\{b\}$, and $\{a, b\}$, respectively, as their CAT's (e.g., S_1 and S_2 are two different employees, and S_3 is their manager), and one object called O (e.g., a business document). Since each subject is either allowed or denied access to O, the total number of all possible access patterns of these three subjects to O is eight. By specifying $ACE(O)$ appropriately, it can be shown (Figure 4) that any of these eight access patterns can be precisely enforced by the $BEAC$ model.

Subject	Category Set
S_1	{ a }
S_2	{ b }
S_3	{ a, b }

ACE of O	S_1	S_2	S_3
< a >	X		X
< b >		X	X
< a + b >	X	X	X
< a * b >			X
< $\overline{a}$ >		X	
< $\overline{b}$ >	X		
< $\overline{a} + \overline{b}$ >	X	X	
< $\overline{a} * \overline{b}$ >			

Figure 4.2. The eight access patterns of three subjects and their enforcement. An "X" in the entry means that subject S_i can access object O with the corresponding ACE.

4.5 Relationship to Multilevel Security

In this section the relationship, in terms of modeling power[1], between conventional multilevel security models and the *BEAC* model is discussed. Theoretically, a multilevel security model with solely non-hierarchical categories is powerful enough to enforce any security policy which is enforced by a multilevel model with only hierarchical levels. This can be easily proved by mapping the lattice of security levels into another lattice consisting of only security categories in such a way that whenever a level L_i is directly dominated by another level L_j, L_i and L_j are mapped to two category sets C_i and C_j, respectively, such that $C_i \subset C_j$. (The easiest way to achieve this mapping is to add a new category to C_i to form C_j).

---

[1]The power of a model is defined as its capability of enforcing security policies. Model A is more powerful than model B if all the security policies which B can enforce is a proper subset of the security policies that A can enforce.

After showing that non-categories categories are more powerful than hierarchical levels in enforcing security policies, we further claim that the *BEAC* model has at least the same power in policy enforcement as the multilevel security model with categories, that is, the former can enforce any security policy that the latter can enforce.

Theorem 1 *Any security policy which can be enforced by a lattice-based multilevel security model with only categories can also be enforced by the BEAC model.*

Proof:

Suppose that a security policy is to be enforced in a system comprising subjects and objects by multilevel security with only categories, and data confidentiality is the main security concern, then a subject has read access to an object only when the category set of the subject contains that of the object, and a subject has write access to an object only when the category set of the subject is contained by that of the object. We will show how to transfer the security attributes of subjects and objects in this multilevel model to the security attributes used by the *BEAC* model such that the same security policy can still be enforced.

To enforce the security policy by the *BEAC* model, all the subjects still keep exactly the same category set as they had as above, but the ACEs of each object need to be defined according to its original category set. Since there are two access modes (read and write) allowed on each object in multilevel security, two ACEs are required for each object. If the original category set of an object O is $\{c_1, c_2, \cdots, c_i\}$, then its *ACE* for read access will be defined as $< c_1 * c_2 * \cdots * c_i >$, since in order to read O, a subject must have each one of $c_1, c_2, \cdots, c_i$ in its category set. The ACE of O_k for write access will be defined as $< (c_1 + c_2 + \cdots + c_i) * \overline{\$} >$, since to write O, a subject may have only a subset of $\{c_1, c_2, \cdots, c_i\}$ in its category set but contains no other categories.

Defining the ACEs for both read and write operations of each object in this way, security policies for all objects are exactly preserved as enforced by the original multilevel model with categories. Therefore, it is claimed that the $BEAC$ model is at least as powerful as multilevel security with categories. $\diamond$

Because of the transitivity property of security models' power in policy enforcement, the $BEAC$ model can also enforce any security policy enforced by the multilevel security model with hierarchical levels. However, the categories used in the $BEAC$ model has a more similar meanings as the categories in multilevel security, thus in practice $BEAC$ can be used in parallel with the conventional multilevel model with only levels. That is, the security attribute of each subject and object can contain a security level in addition to a CAT and $ACEs$, respectively Access to an object is allowed when both the level comparison test and the boolean evaluation test pass.

In effect, it can be further shown that the $BEAC$ model possesses a greater power in enforcing security policies than a multilevel security model with categories, as explained by the proof of the following theorem.

**Theorem 2** _There exist security policies which can be enforced by the BEAC model but cannot by a multilevel security model with categories._

Proof:

The theorem can be easily proved by providing an example of such a security policy. Suppose a system contains two subjects, S_1 and S_2, and two objects O_1 and O_2, and a security policy is to be enforced such that all the allowable and disallowed accesses to objects by subjects are shown in Figure 2. Both subjects can write information to both objects, but only S_1 can read information from O_1 and only S_2 can read information from O_2. An application which might need this policy is that S_1 acts as a processing filter for O_1 such that any information written to O_1 must be read and processed by S_1 before it can be written to other objects again. S_2 plays the same role to O_2. Another application is that O_1 is the mailbox of S_1 and O_2 is the mailbox of S_2. Any subject may send messages to any mailbox but only the owner of a mailbox can read information from it.

First, we show how this security policy can be enforced by the $BEAC$ model. S_1 and S_2 are assigned category sets $\{a\}$ and $\{b\}$, respectively. O_1 can be written by both S_1 and S_2 but can be read only by S_1, thus $ACE(O_1)_W = <a+b>$ and $ACE(O_1)_R = <a \star \overline{b}>$. O_2 can be written by both S_1 and S_2 but can be read only by S_2, thus $ACE(O_2)_W = <a+b>$ and $ACE(O_2)_R = <\overline{a} \star b>$.

Then let us try to enforce Figure 2 by multilevel security with a security class containing only categories. Since S_1 can both read and write O_1, $class(S_1) = class(O_1)$. Similarly, since S_2 can both read and write O_2, $class(S_2) = class(O_2)$. Moreover, since S_2 can write but cannot read O_1, the category set of O_1 must properly contain the category set of S_2 (again, assume data confidentiality is the security

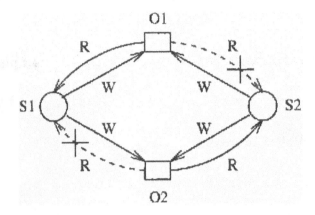

Figure 4.3. An access control policy which can be enforced by the *BEAC* model but cannot by a multilevel security model with categories.

concern), i.e., $class(O_1) \supset class(S_2)$, which implies $class(S_1) \supset class(S_2)$. However, with the same reasoning, the category set of O_2 must properly contain the category set of S_1, i.e., $class(O_2) \supset class(S_1)$, which implies $class(S_2) \supset class(S_1)$, that contradicts the previous implication. Therefore, this security policy cannot be possibly enforced by a multilevel security model with categories. ◊

As an observation from the proof above, it is concluded that any security policy whose *allowable information flow graph* contains a cycle consisting of read and write edges among more than two system entities (e.g., $O_1 \rightarrow S_1 \rightarrow O_2 \rightarrow S_2 \rightarrow O_1$ in Figure 2), cannot be enforced by a lattice-based access control model.

4.6   Enforcement of Complex Security Policies with *BEAC*

4.6.1   Enforcing Multilevel Exceptions

In Section 4.2, multilevel information flow exceptions are categorized in terms of access control and justified by the security requirements of different applications.

It is now shown that how these exceptions can be enforced by the $BEAC$ model. For clarity, all the security policies mentioned in this section use the following conventions:

- $S_1, S_2, S_3, \cdots$: each represents a subject.

- $O_1, O_2, O_3, \cdots$: each represents an object.

- $CAT(S_i)$: the category set of subject S_i.

- $ACE(O_j)_M$: the access control expression of object O_j for access mode M.

- $A, B, C, \cdots$: each represents a set of categories.

- $p, q, r, \cdots$: each represents a reusable category in the CAT of a subject or a non-persistent category in the ACE of an object.

- $\hat{p}, \hat{q}, \hat{r}, \cdots$: each represents a one-time category in the CAT of a subject or a persistent category in the ACE of an object.

- $E, F, G, \cdots$: each represents a boolean expression.

Implementations of the six multilevel exceptions defined in Figure 4-1 are shown as follows:

[i] transitivity exception - integrity

Initially, the security attributes of subjects and objects are assumed to be:

$CAT(S_1) = \{A\},$

$ACE(O_1)_W = < E_1 >,$

$$ACE(O_1)_R = <E_2>,$$

$$CAT(S_2) = \{B\},$$

$$ACE(O_2)_W = <F>,$$

where category set A makes E_1 TRUE, and category set B makes both E_2 and F TRUE. If the access patterns are regulated with a lattice-based multilevel security model, S_1 should be allowed to directly write O_2, according to the transitivity property. In order to preserve this property in the $BEAC$ model, A will also make F TRUE. However, if an exception to this property is desired, attributes of subjects and objects can be changed as the following:

$$CAT(S_1) = \{A, p\},$$

$$ACE(O_1)_W = <E_1 * p>,$$

$$ACE(O_1)_R = <E_2 * q>,$$

$$CAT(S_2) = \{B, q\},$$

$$ACE(O_2)_W = <F * q>,$$

where p and q are different categories and do not appear in any of A, B, E_1, E_2, or F. Modifying the security attributes of these subjects and objects in this way, the original allowable access patterns among them are still maintained except the write access of S_1 to O_2. Since q does not exist in $CAT(S_1)$, S_1 will not be able to write O_2 directly any more.

[ii] transitivity exception - confidentiality

Similar to the previous case, we assume the original security attributes of subjects and objects as:

$$ACE(O_1)_R = < E >,$$

$$CAT(S_1) = \{A\},$$

$$ACE(O_2)_W = < F_1 >,$$

$$ACE(O_2)_R = < F_2 >,$$

$$CAT(S_2) = \{B\},$$

where A makes both E and F_1 TRUE, and B makes F_2 TRUE. If the access patterns are regulated with a lattice-based multilevel security model, S_2 should be allowed to directly read O_1, according to the transitivity property. In order to preserve this property in the $BEAC$ model, B will also make E TRUE. However, if an exception to this property is desired, the security attributes of subjects and objects can be changed as the following:

$$ACE(O_1)_R = < E * p >,$$

$$CAT(S_1) = \{A, p\},$$

$$ACE(O_2)_W = < F_1 * p >,$$

$$ACE(O_2)_R = < F_2 * q >,$$

$$CAT(S_2) = \{B, q\},$$

where categories p and q do not occur in any of A, B, E_1, E_2, or F. Now the original allowable access patterns among them are still maintained except the read access of

S_2 to O_1, because $CAT(S_2)$ cannot make $ACE(O_2)_W$ TRUE now.

[iii] aggregation exception - integrity

The original security attributes of subjects and objects are assumed to be:

$$CAT(S_1) = \{A\},$$

$$CAT(S_2) = \{B\},$$

$$ACE(O_3)_W = < E >,$$

where A and B are two category sets which both make E TRUE (note that A and B are not necessarily distinct). If an aggregation exception is desired to be enforced between S_1 and S_2 to O_3, their security attributes can be changed as the following:

$$CAT(S_1) = \{A, p\},$$

$$CAT(S_2) = \{B, q\},$$

$$ACE(O_3)_W = < E * (\bar{\hat{p}} + \bar{\hat{q}}) >,$$

where both p and q are newly created. Since persistent categories $\hat{p}$ and $\hat{q}$ are complemented in the new ACE, they actually simulate a lock which is open to any subject unless the subject has both keys p and q. (So changing the ACE of O_3 this way will not affect the access privileges of other subjects.) Initially, O_3 can be written by either S_1 or S_2 because a single p or q still can make $ACE(O_3)_W$ TRUE. After S_1, for example, writes O_3, the value of $\hat{p}$ in $ACE(O_3)_W$ will remain 1, which makes the ACE equivalent to $< E * \bar{\hat{q}} >$. When S_2 then tries to write O_3, the ACE will be evaluated FALSE due to the category q in $CAT(S_2)$, so its access attempt will be denied. (However, S_1 is still allowed to access O_3)

[iv] aggregation exception - confidentiality

The original security attributes of subjects and objects are assumed to be:

$$ACE(O_1)_R =< E >,$$

$$ACE(O_2)_R =< F >,$$

$$CAT(S_3) = \{A\},$$

where A is a category set which makes both E and F TRUE (note that E and F are not necessarily distinct). To enforce an aggregation exception between O_1 and O_2 for their read accesses to S_3, their security attributes can be changed as the following:

$$ACE(O_1)_R =< E * (\hat{p} + \bar{r}) >,$$

$$ACE(O_2)_R =< F * (\hat{p} + \bar{r}) >,$$

$$CAT(S_3) = \{A, \mathring{p}, r\},$$

where p is a new category just created, and appears as a one-time category in $CAT(S_3)$ and as a persistent category in the ACEs of both objects. The category r is also brand new and the purpose of complementing it in the ACEs of O_1 and O_2 is to remove the effects on other unrelated subjects' privileges resulting from the enforcement of an aggregation exception between both objects for S_3. Any other subject which originally has access to O_1 or O_2 can still access it, since r does not exist in its category set. However, r is added to $CAT(S_3)$ so that the $\bar{r}$ in either $ACE(O_1)_R$ or $ACE(O_2)_R$ does not open any door to S_3. Initially, S_3 can read either O_1 or O_2. After S_3 read O_1, for example, the value of $\hat{p}$ in $ACE(O_1)_R$ remains 1, which actually makes the ACE change back to $< E >$. On the other hand, $\hat{p}$ is deleted from $ACE(O_3)$ after its first use, so now $CAT(S_3) = \{A, r\}$, which makes S_3 unable to read O_2 (but stile able to read O_1) .

[v] separation exception - integrity

The original security attributes of subjects and objects and their properties are assumed to be the same as the those assumed in case [iii] (aggregation exception - integrity). If a separation exception is to be enforced between S_1 and S_2 for the write access to O_3, their security attributes will be changed to:

$$CAT(S_1) = \{A, \hat{p}, r\},$$

$$CAT(S_2) = \{B, \hat{p}, r\},$$

$$ACE(O_3)_W = < E * (p * r + \bar{r}) >,$$

where both p and r are just created on demand. The new category r in the ACE of O_3 is again used to invalidate the effect of changing $ACE(O_3)$ for enforcing exception upon the access privileges of other unrelated subjects to O_3. Both S_1 and S_2 also need r to make the first term $(p * r)$ TRUE when they access O_3 at the first time. The one-time category $\hat{p}$ in both $CAT(S_1)$ and $CAT(S_2)$ makes each of them only have write access to O_3 once (the key to open the lock will be lost after its first use). Initially, O_3 can be written by either subject, but once it is written by one subject it can only be written by the other.

[vi] separation exception - confidentiality

The original security attributes of subjects and objects and their properties are assumed to be the same as the those assumed in case [iv] (aggregation exception - confidentiality). If a separation exception is to be enforced between O_1 and O_2 for S_3's read accesses, their security attributes will be changed to:

$$ACE(O_1)_R = < E * (p + \bar{r}) >,$$

$$ACE(O_2)_R = < F * (q + \bar{r}) >,$$

$$CAT(S_3) = \{A, \hat{p}, \hat{q}, r\},$$

where p, q and r are all new. Category r is utilized for the same purpose as above. Initially, S_3 can read either O_1 (with $\hat{p}$) or O_2 (with $\hat{q}$). After S_3 read O_1, for example, it will lose $\hat{p}$ and make itself unable to read O_1 again since category p is non-persistent in $ACE(O_1)_R$. Therefore, S_3 can then be only allowed to read O_2.

From the implementations of aggregation and separation exceptions, we know that the access privileges of other unrelated subjects to the same objects involved in an exception enforcement can be made unaffected by adding a complemented category ($\bar{r}$) to the ACEs of objects and a non-complemented category (r) to the CATs of subjects involved in exception enforcement. If the subjects which originally have accesses to the objects are all involved in the exception enforcement, this technique (of using $\bar{r}$) does not have to be considered in modifying their security attributes. For the enforcement of transitivity exceptions, this technique was not considered, however, can be similarly adopted if necessary.

4.6.2   Specifying a Sequence of Accesses

After elucidating how multilevel exceptions can be enforced effectively by the $BEAC$ model, we now demonstrate another advantage of this model, namely, its ability to assign a sequence of accesses to an object by a number of subjects. For simplicity, the effect of modifying the ACE of an object upon access privileges of other unrelated subjects is not considered.

Consider the simplest case in which two subjects S_1 and S_2 can access (in some mode) an object O_3. Their initial security attributes are assumed as:

$$CAT(S_1) = \{A\},$$

$$CAT(S_2) = \{B\},$$

$$ACE(O_3)_M = <E>,$$

where A and B are two category sets which each makes E TRUE and the subscript M of $ACE(O_3)$ represents the access mode for which we desire to order S_1 and S_2. If we desire to give preference to S_1 such that S_1 must access O_3 first before S_2 can access it, their security attributes can be changed to:

$$CAT(S_1) = \{A, \hat{p}\},$$

$$CAT(S_2) = \{B, \hat{q}\},$$

$$ACE(O_3)_M = <E * (p + \hat{p} * q)>,$$

where new categories p and q do not appear in any of A, B, or E. In $ACE(O_3)_M$, a new boolean expression is ANDed with E such that only S_1 can access O_3 at first.

After S_1's access, tbe ACE of O_3 actually becomes $< E * (p + q) >$, which disables S_1's access to O_3 again because $\hat{p}$ is removed from $CAT(S_1)$. and makes O_3 accessible only to S_2. Tbis idea is in fact very straightforward if we conceive it with tbe lock-key concept. The access right of S_2 to O_3 depends on a complex lock $(\hat{p} * q)$ which must be opened partly by S_1 first. Because tbe lock $(\hat{p})$ opened by S_1 is persistent, S_2 docs not need a key $\hat{p}$ wben it accesses O_3 (actually it cannot have one, otherwise it can access O_3 before S_1).

The idea can be generalized to specify an access sequence to an object O_4 among three subjects S_1, S_2, and S_3. Again, their original security attributes are assumed as:

$$CAT(S_1) = \{A\},$$

$$CAT(S_2) = \{B\},$$

$$CAT(S_3) = \{C\},$$

$$ACE(O_4)_M = < E >,$$

where A, B, and C all make E TRUE. If we desire to specify an access ordering as $S_1 \rightarrow S_2 \rightarrow S_3$, their security attributes can be cbanged to:

$$CAT(S_1) = \{A, \hat{p}\},$$

$$CAT(S_2) = \{B, \hat{q}\},$$

$$CAT(S_3) = \{C, \hat{r}\},$$

$$ACE(O_4)_M = < E * (p + \hat{p} * q + \hat{q} * r) >,$$

wbere new categories p, q, and r do not appear in any of A, B, C, or E. It can be easily verified that at first only S_1 is allowed to access O_4. After S_1's access, tbe ACE

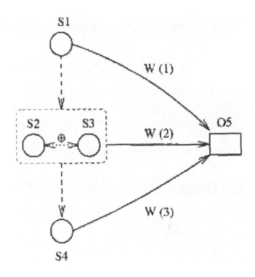

Figure 4.4. A complex security policy requiring both an access ordering and an aggregation exception for integrity.

of O_4 becomes $< E * (p + q + \hat{q} * r) >$, which allows only S_2 to access O_4. Then, after

S_2's access, the ACE of O_4 becomes $< E * (p + q + r) >$, which only allows the access

to O_4 by S_3.

Apparently, the idea used in these two examples can be generalized to order the

accesses to an object by an arbitrary number of subjects.

4.6.3   Combination of Enforcement Techniques

Some complex security policies may require both exception and ordering. The

following shows an example of the $BEAC$ model using these techniques combined.

Again, the effect of modifying the ACE of an object upon access privileges of other

unrelated subjects is not considered but could be eliminated using the technique

mentioned earlier. Assume there is a business application whose security requirement

demands both an access ordering and an aggregation exception, as shown in Figure

4.4.

An object O_5 needs to be written by S_1 first, and then written by either S_2 or S_3 but not both, and finally written by S_4. Assume their original security attributes are:

$$CAT(S_1) = \{A\},$$

$$CAT(S_2) = \{B_1\},$$

$$CAT(S_3) = \{B_2\},$$

$$CAT(S_4) = \{C\},$$

$$ACE(O_5)_W = < E >,$$

where A, B_1, B_2, and C all make E TRUE. To enforce the security policy, we need to use both the technique of specifying an access sequence among S_1, $[S_2 + S_3]$ (to treat them as one entity), and S_4 and the technique of achieving an aggregation exception for data integrity between S_2 and S_3. Therefore, the security attributes become:

$$CAT(S_1) = \{A, \hat{p}\},$$

$$CAT(S_2) = \{B_1, \hat{q}, \hat{s}\},$$

$$CAT(S_3) = \{B_2, \hat{q}, \hat{t}\},$$

$$CAT(S_4) = \{C, \hat{r}\},$$

$$ACE(O_5)_M = < E * (p + \hat{p} * q * (\bar{\hat{s}} + \bar{\hat{t}}) + \hat{q} * r) >,$$

where new categories p, q, r, s, and t do not appear in any of A, B_1, B_2, C, or E. Initially only S_1 can write O_5, and after S_1 writes, $ACE(O_5)_M = < E * (p + q * (\bar{\hat{s}} + \bar{\hat{t}}) + \hat{q} * r) >$, which only allows either S_2 or S_3 to write O_5. If S_2 writes, $ACE(O_5)_M = < E * (p + q * \bar{\hat{t}} + r) >$, then only S_4 can write O_5. If S_3 writes, $ACE(O_5)_M = < E * (p + q * \bar{\hat{s}} + r) >$, and still only S_4 can write O_5.

4.7   Implementation of BEAC

In order to demonstrate the practicability of *BEAC*, the model has been implemented as a client-server access control system. A centralized access control server approach is assumed such that the security attributes of all entities including CATs and passwords of subjects and ACEs of objects are managed by an access control server module and only the users playing the roles of system security administrators are allowed to access the files storing these security attributes (which means only the administrators can specify the security policy, a mandatory access control flavor).

The client module is a C program providing an interface to let a user (subject) communicate with the access control server to try to obtain access to an object. When a user runs a client program, a simple password-checking mechanism (without encryption) is first used to authenticate the user before any access attempt from a user can be initiated. If the authentication is valid, the user then specifies the name of the object that the user would like to access in a request to the access control server, and gets back a response indicating the authorization decision. Although multiple client processes can run simultaneously, for safety and reliability, currently the server is programmed to handle a single client at a time.

The access control server is just a software implementation of *BEAC* with C language. It accepts two kinds of requests from a client process, one for authentication of users, and the other for authorization of object accesses. Therefore, it only responds with a yes/no answer to any request from the client. The access control rule for evaluating the *ACE* of an object using the *CAT* of a subject and the attribute updating rule for modifying the security attributes after an access trial are both implemented within this module.

To avoid the burden of manipulating low-level communication primitives (e.g., *socket*), communications between a client and the server are achieved using Sun's *Remote Procedure Call* (RPC) and *eXternal Data Representation* (XDR). XDR is a standard way of encoding data in a portable fashion between different systems and thus can be used to define the interfaces of all remote procedure calls in *BEAC*. The Sun's RPC compiler, *RPCGEN*, is used to take the files specified with XDR to generate the source code of a client *stub* and a server *stub*, in which low-level procedure call functions are offered. To make executable server and client modules, the client stub and the server stub are compiled and linked with the object code of a server program and a client program, respectively. When both modules are run, the client can call a procedure remotely existed in the server just like a local procedure call. All communication details are handled by the underlying RPC system.

In practical distributed systems, a client should make an access request to an object server in order to access an object, and the object server consults the access control server where all security information are centralized to see if the access should be allowed or denied. Therefore, there will be two recursive remote procedure calls involved in one access. Since the current goal of implementing *BEAC* is to show that the model is implementable and has practical values, only a simplified system is adopted.

CHAPTER 5
ACCESS CONTROL WITH EXTENDED CAPABILITIES

5.1 Motivation

Most existing capability-based systems only enforce static access control policies. When an object server receives a capability from a subject for accessing an object under its management, it simply verifies the validity of the capability, and if the capability has never been subject to tampering, the subject is granted the access rights placed on the capability. However, as seen in the previous chapters, many complex security policies are state-dependent. That is, an access authorization often depends not only on the subject's access history and but also on the object's history of being accessed. This type of dynamic access control policies is difficult to enforce using the conventional ticket-type capability schemes, without resorting to additional access control mechanisms. The concept of access control lists certainly could be utilized for the enforcement of complex security policies due to its centralized feature. Yet, using centralized access control lists excessively apparently loses the advantages of using capabilities in distributed systems. Accordingly, an extension of the capability system to handle complex and diversified security requirements is justified.

This chapter proposes an *extended capability* system [44], which provides additional functions to enforce many complex access control requirements. The innovative

79

idea is to place complicated and tedious access control information on the extended capabilities distributed to subjects and to keep only simple and regulated capability processing rules and relatively little access information about objects at the object servers. After the basics of an extended capability are introduced in the next section, three practical policies are used to demonstrate how complex access meditation can be achieved by this new capability system in section 3. Moreover, some capability management issues which include propagation, revocation, and distribution of extended capabilities are elaborated in section 4.

5.2   Extended Capability

This section introduces the format of an extended capability and how it is generated. Prior to that, the system environment that the extended capabilities are to be used is first described.

5.2.1   System Environment

An object-oriented system model is assumed. Each object in the system is encapsulated and managed by an object server. A request to access an object is serviced by its object server which actually performs the access operation on behalf of the accessing subject. Each access request is authorized by an extended capability associated with the object, presented by the subject. The object server is responsible for all the processing regarding extended capabilities including generation, distribution, verification, and revocation of capabilities. The object server is assumed to be a part of the trusted computing base (TCB), which guarantees that the server cannot be bypassed for any access attempt and always work as desired in executing access

subject	rights	lifetime	ACI	check

subject   - The "id" and "type" of the subject who owns the capability

rights   - Access rights with bit pattern depending on the type of the object

lifetime   - The time when the capability expires

ACI   - Access control information sepcified by the access control server

check   - Bit field for protecting the capability from forgery

Figure 5.1. The format of an *E-cap*

operations. For brevity, an extended capability described below will be named an *E-cap*.

5.2.2 Format of an *E-cap*

The format of an *E-cap* and the meanings of all the fields contained are shown in Figure 1. Like an identity-based capability, an *E-cap* can only be used by the *subject* specified in the capability. Thus, if a suitable authentication mechanism is employed for authorization in the system, a malicious subject cannot gain access to an object with a stolen *E-cap*. The *subject* field is further divided into two subfields, the *id* and *type* of the subject. The *rights* field of an *E-cap* determines the access privileges that the *subject* possesses to an object, and its interpretation depends upon the type of the object. An *E-cap* also has a *lifetime* field which tells when the capability will expire, based on the local clock of the object server. An *ACI* field is included in an *E-cap*, to store important access control information by an object server. It provides the primary information for enforcing complex security policies. This field also has different meanings for different types of objects and different policies, and is only recognizable to the object server. The last field of an *E-cap*, *check*, is used to protect the capability from forgery or tampering, and the determination of its value is discussed immediately below.

5.2.3 Generation of an *E-cap*

Each object in an *E-cap* capability system is associated with a unique secret number, called *seed*, known only to the object server managing the object. The main purpose of the *seed* number is to prevent capability forgery and to facilitate full capability revocation. The secrecy of the *seed* number is crucial to a capability system, and therefore must be fully protected by the object server.

An *E-cap* is created upon the request of a subject to an object server, which then consults the *access control server*, also a trusted component in the system, where all access control information are stored in some pre-determined way. The access control server first determines the values of all fields except the *check* in the *E-cap*, according to the security policy to be enforced. These values are then passed to the object server which computes the *check* field to complete the construction of the *E-cap*. The *check* field is computed by using a publicly known one-way function as follows:

$$check = f(subject, seed, rights, lifetime, ACI)$$

It is actually a signature of the object server on an *E-cap* before it is issued to a subject, and this field will be examined each time the *E-cap* is presented to the server later.

The principle of separating policy and mechanism is thus achieved by having an access control server which also provides user interface for specifying security policies in addition to translating policies into the fields of *E-cap*'s. On the other hand, an object server acts only as a mechanism for access enforcement according the information placed on the capabilities. The access control server needs to be consulted only once before any accesses.

Before other problems about the management of *E-cap*'s are discussed, we first elaborate how an *E-cap* system can be used to mediate accesses from subjects to objects, beyond the traditional ticket-like scheme.

5.3   Access Mediation with an *E-Cap* System

When an *E-cap* is presented to an object server along with a request to access an object, the server first needs to check whether the *E-cap* has ever been tampered by recomputing the *check* field. Only the subject which presents an *E-cap* owned by itself, with a correct *check* field will "possibly" gain access rights shown on the capability. Then the object server utilizes the information stored in the *ACI* field to determine whether the access attempt should be allowed or denied. We now show several ways to utilize this field to enforce frequently required access control policies.

5.3.1   Strongly Typed Systems

In a strongly typed system, every subject and object has a type associated with it and its type cannot be changed discretionally. The type of a subject usually represents the role or class of the subject, and each type often implies a different set of access privileges. The type of an object expresses the category of the information stored in the object.

One *E-cap* for all the subjects of the same type

The access patterns of many applications may have the property that all the subjects of one type share the same set of access rights to an object. For example, all the faculty in a department have "read" and "write" rights to the department's "Technical_Report_List" file, but all the students have only a "read" right to that file. Since the *subject* field of an *E-cap* contains a *type* subfield, we can use it to generalize an *E-cap* such that all the subjects in one type can use the same *E-cap* to access the object. When such a capability is created, the *id* part in *subject* is set all 0's and the *type* of those subjects is specified. The *ACI* field is configured to indicate that this *E-cap* is a *typed* one, thus an access request will be allowed as long as the accessing subject belongs to the *type* and the access operation needs only the *rights*, both specified in the *E-cap*.

A typed *E-cap* has storage advantage since it can be shared by all the subjects of the same type, thus the need of memory space for storing one capability for each subject is diminished. Alternatively, it can be freely copied from one subject to the other subjects of the same type, so the workload of generating capabilities for all the subjects, especially when the number of subjects in that type is large, at the access control server, can be significantly reduced. To support such a typed *E-cap*, the authentication service needs to ensure that an object server get the correct type of an accessing subject, a requirement easily achievable by just including the type information of a subject in the authentication message.

One *E-cap* for all the objects of the same type

Similarly, in a strongly typed system there exist applications requiring that a subject has the same access rights to all the objects of the same type. For example, a professor may have "execute" rights for all the executable files of the "Student_Project" type, and a student has "read" rights for all the files of type "Project_Assignment". To make things easier in such cases, we wish that a subject could use only one capability to access all the objects in the same type. In order to achieve this, the *seed* number associated with an object is augmented to contain two seed numbers, one for the object itself (called *id_seed*) and the other for the type of the object (called *type_seed*). The *id_seed* is still unique to each object, yet all the objects of the same type share the same *type_seed*. When an *E-cap* is created, it is the *type_seed* that is used in computing the *check* field with the one-way function, and the *ACI* field is configured to indicate such a capability preparation. Later, when this *E-cap* is presented to an object server, the *subject* can use it to access any object in the same type with the *rights* specified in the capability. This technique not only reduces the computation overhead of generating one capability for each object in the same type by the object server, but also saves memory space required to store capabilities by subjects.

5.3.2   Implementation of N-time Tickets

Some applications may require that a group of subjects can only access a particular object for a certain number of times. That is, each subject in the group has a pre-determined number of times to access an object and will not be able to access the object after all of its allowed accesses are performed. A special case of this policy is a one-time ticket, by which each subject in a group can only access an object only once. It is apparent that many activities in the real world need this feature. Therefore, we first show how such an access control requirement can be enforced by an E-cap system.

Implementing one-time tickets

Implementing a one-time ticket for each subject in a group can be achieved by using a salient feature of prime numbers, which has been employed to reduce the overhead of manipulating access control lists [58]. Assume the group consists of k subjects, represented as $S_1, S_2, \cdots, S_k$, and each of them will be given an E-cap that can be used only once to access an object O. This can be fulfilled by storing a unique prime p_i in the ACI field of the capability given to S_i, and storing a number $prod(O)$, which is the product of all primes (i.e., $prod(O) = p_1 \cdot p_2 \cdots p_k$), with O. When an S_i attempts to access O with its E-cap, the number $prod(O)$ will be divided by p_i. If it is divisible, the access request of S_i will be granted and the resulting quotient will become the new $prod(O)$. If not, the access request of S_i will be denied and nothing changes. Due to the property of primes, $prod(O)$ can be divisible by each p_i only once, which exactly renders a one-time access of O to each S_i.

After all S_i's have accessed O, $prod(O)$ becomes 1. If desired, $prod(O)$ can be reset to the initial product number, also as advised by some processing rule in the object server, thus making each one-time E-cap usable one more time. Another advantage of this scheme is its flexibility, in that a new subject S_{k+1} can be added to the group at any time, as long as it is given an E-cap with the ACI containing a unique prime p_{k+1} and the current $prod(O)$ is multiplied by p_{k+1}. Similarly, a subject S_i can also be removed from the group at any time, by just dividing $prod(O)$ by p_i.

Extension to n-time tickets

The technique of implementing one-time tickets for a group of subjects to access an object can be extended to a more general case, n-time tickets. That is, each subject S_i is allowed to access O for n_i times, $1 \leq i \leq k$, where each n_i is not necessarily the same. For this case, each S_i is still given an E-cap with a unique prime p_i in its ACI, but the $prod(O)$ with object O is computed initially as

$$prod(O) = p_1^{n_1} \cdot p_2^{n_2} \cdots p_k^{n_k}$$

The same division operation is performed when subject S_i presents its E-cap to the object server along with its access request. Because of the property of primes, $prod(O)$ can be divisible by p_i for only n_i times, which means the E-cap of S_i is valid for only n_i times of accesses. For example, a group of three subjects S_1, S_2, and S_3 can access object O for three, one, and two times, respectively. Assume $p_1 = 2$, $p_2 = 3$, $p_3 = 5$, then initially $prod(O) = p_1^{n_1} \cdot p_2^{n_2} \cdot p_3^{n_3} = 2^3 \cdot 3^1 \cdot 5^2 = 600$. After S_3 accesses O

once, $prod(O)$ becomes $\frac{600}{5} = 120$. After S_1 accesses O twice later, $prod(O)$ becomes $\frac{120}{2^2} = 30$, which leaves each S_i only one time of access. In addition to possessing the same advantage as for one-time tickets, this more general scheme is even more powerful and flexible in that it allows the object server, according to the requirements of applications, to dynamically increase or decrease the number of times a subject can access an object at any time, by appropriately adjusting the value of $prod(O)$.

To implement the n-time tickets for object O, the object server needs to be equipped with some capability processing rules and mechanisms (e.g., generating prime numbers, dividing $prod(O)$ by p_i), but only a $prod(O)$ and a index indicating the largest prime used up to now need to be kept for the object.

5.3.3 Enforcing Access Sequences

Many business applications have the security requirement that a set of related subjects need to access an object in a specific sequence with probably different access rights. The E-cap system can also support such a requirement with additional functions added to the object server. The idea is to give each subject a different E-cap such that a capability can be used to access the object only if each subject strictly follows the pre-determined access sequence. Instead of elaborating how this scheme works generally, an example is used to demonstrate the idea.

Generating capabilities

Let's assume that an object O needs to be accessed by three subjects with different access rights, in a sequence as $S_1 \rightarrow S_2 \rightarrow S_3$. When this access control policy is specified through the access control service, an access sequence number (ASN) is assigned to this particular policy. When the object server of O generates capabilities for this policy, this ASN will be stored in the ACI field of the E-cap given to each subject. In addition to the one-way function used to compute the check field in an E-cap, another one-way function is used by the object server to simulate the change of the seed number of O for a specific access sequence. These two one-way functions are distinct since their input parameters are different.

1. $f_{check}()$: is the original one-way function to compute the check field, in order to prevent capability forgery.

2. $f_{stem}()$: is used to obtain a new stem number from the ASN and from either the seed or the current stem number of O.

To generate an E-cap C_1 for S_1, a number called $stem_1$ is first obtained by

$$f_{stem}(seed, ASN) = stem_1$$

After all direct information are put into C_1, the check field is computed based on $stem_1$:

$$f_{check}(S_1, stem_1, rights_1, lifetime_1, ACI_1) = check_1$$

Then, to generate an E-cap C_2 for S_2, a number called $stem_2$ is obtained from the $stem_1$ and ASN as

$$f_{stem}(stem_1, ASN) = stem_2$$

and the check field of C_2 is determined based on this new stem number by

$$f_{check}(S_2, stem_2, rights_2, lifetime_2, ACI_2) = check_2$$

Finally, the check field of C_3 for S_3 is determined by the following computations

$$f_{stem}(stem_2, ASN) = stem_3$$

$$f_{check}(S_3, stem_3, rights_3, lifetime_3, ACI_3) = check_3$$

Notice that all the C_i's contain the same ASN in their ACI fields.

Access restriction

When S_1 presents its C_1 for accessing O, the object server of O will first extract the ASN from its ACI field to compute $stem_1$. Then the same check field verification procedure is performed with the replacement of the seed number by $stem_1$ in verification. Since only C_1 will contain a correct check field, only S_1 is allowed to access O. All other C_i's will not be verified as valid ones at this time, since their check fields are computed based upon different stem numbers. After the access of S_1, $stem_2$ is computed using $f_{check}()$ from $stem_1$ and ASN, and becomes the seed number in the next verification of the check field. Similarly, $stem_3$ will be computed to replace $stem_2$ and play the same role after the access of S_2.

It is quite obvious that each subject must follow the specified sequence in order to access O, because each C_i will not be treated as a valid one if it is not used at the right time. The number *stem*, is utilized as a *virtual seed* number of O *for this particular access sequence.* This number is modified immediately after the access of S_i, to make C_i just used invalid, and to make the object server only accept C_{i+1}, which allows no subjects but S_{i+1} to access O next.

Some applications may require that an access sequence repeat after the access of the last subject in the sequence. For example, a daily routine task needs a group of users to access a file in a fixed order everyday. This can be accomplished by storing additional information in the *ACI* field of the *E-cap* of the last subject, to advise the object server to remove the current stem number after all accesses in a sequence are finished.

Elimination of storing the *stem* number

The scheme for enforcing an access sequence described above is also storage efficient since only one *stem* number needs to be stored for each policy, and more favorably, it will not be produced until the access of the first subject in the sequence. Indeed, even the necessity of storing this number can be released at the cost of additional computation at each access. The access order of each subject in the sequence can also be specified in the *ACI* field of its *E-cap*. Thus, each stem number is generated from the *seed* number and the order information in the *E-cap*. With the example used above, $stem_2$ can be generated by calling $f_{check}()$ twice when C_2 is presented by S_2.

5.4 Capability Management

It has been demonstrated that an *E-cap* system is capable of enforcing a number of complex access control policies with an extensive use of the *ACI* field in the *E-cap*. We now discuss how capabilities can be propagated, revoked, and distributed in an *E-cap* system.

5.4.1 Propagation of Capabilities

Capability propagation is a mechanism to support granting of access rights from one subject to the other. Since the *E-cap* system is identity-based, a subject S_1 who wants to transfer its rights to another subject S_2 needs to explicitly make a request to the object server, along with its own *E-cap*, C_1.

Although it is the security policy that determines whether or not a subject can transfer his rights to another one, the object server can be configured to propagate C_2 to S_2 only when S_1 is the owner of the object (which can be indicated by a "owner" right), when a "transfer" right bit on C_1 is on, or after the object server checks the access control server to see if this right transfer complies with the security policy. All these alternatives can be specified in the *ACI* field when an *E-cap* is generated initially, and thus the object server can refer to this information from the *E-cap* to take appropriate actions when a propagation request is made later.

The propagation tree suggested in the *ICAP* architecture [30] can also be incorporated in our *E-cap* system, yet in a distributed way. Whenever C_2 is propagated to S_2, the *id* of S_1, the subject which invokes the propagation, can be embedded in the *ACI* field of C_2 to record from where it is inherited. A propagation tree can thus be built to keep track of all capability propagations, and the whole tree is actually distributed among the subjects in the system. When there is a need to know how access rights were propagated, we can upward trace the propagation tree by requesting each subject in the tracing path to present its capability in order to find its ancestor. In a general case in which only the owner of an object can transfer access rights, the depth of the tree is just two.

Some typed *E-cap* capabilities can be freely duplicated by a subject and transferred to other subjects of the same type, which results in a reduction of the workload for generating capabilities by the object server.

5.4.2 Revocation of Capabilities

Revocation of capabilities is always a difficult problem in a capability-based system. This problem becomes more troublesome in distributed systems, since all capabilities are distributed among the autonomous subjects for which there exists no centralized authority. While four metrics about the implementation of capability revocation have been discussed in [75], a selective (only selective capabilities are revoked) and partial (only partial rights in a capability are revoked) revocation scheme is often desired by many applications.

When capabilities are manipulated in the user space, they cannot be revoked simply by modifying them with the mechanisms in the system space like the back-pointers implemented in Multics [66]. Besides utilizing an *expire* field to make a capability invalid after a pre-determined time period, there are two general revocation methods including changing the *seed* number associated with an object or maintaining a revocation list suggested by Gong [30]. Changing the *seed* invalidates all the capabilities generated based on this seed, and thus cannot support a selective revocation. With revoked capabilities stored in a revocation list associated with an object, on every access, both the revocation list and the validity of the capability are checked in parallel. In order to avoid the inefficiency caused by searching a long revocation list, a *count* field can be associated with an object to determine how many capabilities have been issued for the object [73]. When the size of the revocation list becomes a significant fraction of the *count*, the object server just performs a permanent revocation by changing the *seed* of the object. However, re-issuing capabilities to subjects based on the new *seed* requires the object server to keep track of the propagation of all the capabilities, which may not be practical as well.

In the *E-cap* system, some capabilities are revoked on purpose in order to enforce a security policy, by changing a virtual seed number associated with the security policy (as in the case of enforcing an access sequence) or using the information in the *ACI* field (as in the case of implementing n-time tickets). Revocation of all the capabilities associated with a particular security policy can also be implemented by maintaining a *policy revocation list* with an object. So when a security policy is not to be enforced any more, all the *E-cap*'s generated for that policy (they should have the same policy number in their *ACI* field) can be made useless by putting the policy number in that revocation list. Part of our future work will be concentrating on how to use the *ACI* field more effectively to support efficient and selective revocation in an *E-cap* system.

5.4.3 Distribution of Capabilities

There are generally two methodologies of how capabilities are distributed to subjects for enforcing the security policy. The first one, adopted or implied by most capability systems [4, 5, 30, 47, 46, 73], is to generate capabilities on demand. That is, a capability is not generated or distributed to a subject until it is needed. As a result, the object server often need to checks the access control server (usually after an object access) to determine the suitable time at which what capabilities should be generated and distributed to whom. The apparent disadvantage of this method is inefficiency in that too frequent checking with the access control server not only violates the original purpose of using capabilities, but very possibly makes the centralized access control server a network and performance bottleneck when the object servers are numerous.

The second methodology, also the one used in our *E-cap* system, is to generate as many capabilities at a time as possible. When a security policy is to be enforced among some subjects, the object server obtains all the necessary information from the access control server to build all the capabilities at a time, and distributes them to the subjects before any actual access operation commences. Although the relations among the capabilities may become more complex (thus the cost of generating capabilities would be a little higher), the overhead of contacting with the access control server subsequently can be diminished considerably. As shown previously, the object server also needs to possess mechanisms to process capabilities and to keep simple access control information for objects, which are usually kept by the access control server in other capability systems. Certainly, there exists some very complex security policies which can hardly be enforced by simply generating all capabilities at a time without consulting the access control server again. However, the strategies of distributing access control information on capabilities earlier and of sharing access enforcement responsibilities with object servers are believed to be effective in balancing storage overhead and enhancing the overall performance of a distributed system.

CHAPTER 6
CONCLUSIONS AND FUTURE WORK

Security has become one of the most important research topics in distributed systems, and more in-depth exploration and investigation into different aspects of computer and network security are needed. In this dissertation work, significant research results have been shown by either enhancing the performance (efficiency) or increasing the power (effectiveness) of the authentication and authorization services and mechanisms. Conclusions of these works and possible future tasks are discussed individually on each research area.

6.1 Authentication and Key Distribution

A new nonce-based authentication protocol which makes use of uncertified keys to reduce its message complexity is proposed. The protocol is formally shown to achieve the authentication goals recommended by BAN. The number of messages required is four for the initial authentication and three for each subsequent repeated authentication, both known to be the minimum of all authentication protocols found in the literature. The protocol can be improved to become more robust against impersonation attacks in later authentications even when session keys are compromised. That improvement is achieved by using an additional one-time key without increasing the number of messages during initial authentication. The protocol is extended further to support repeated authentication. The use of symmetrical storing of session-key certificates is more secure and adaptive to the peer-to-peer communication paradigm in distributed systems. A natural extension of the protocol to a version for inter-domain authentication is also accomplished without the need to modify the authentication mechanisms at local machines. Autonomous determination of using repeated authentication at each level makes the authentication service more flexible and adaptive to the system environment.

Recently, authentication protocol researchers are concentrating on how to effectively use one-way data integrity operations, instead of bulk encryption and decryption operations , for authentication and key distribution, in order to reduce the communication overhead (because the length of authentication messages can be reduced greatly by using a one-way function) and to enhance the performance (since the computation with one-way function is more efficient than encryption and decryption). The authentication protocols proposed in this dissertation can be also explored and modified to accommodate the use of one-way integrity function. In addition, because of the great popularity of commercial applications on World-Wide Web and the relatively low bandwidth of the Internet, the idea of using uncertified keys to reduce message complexity can be applied to different security applications.

6.2 Modeling of Complex Security Policies

An innovative access control model called *BEAC* is proposed to provide a systematic mechanism of modeling human-defined complex security policies by adequately assigning security attributes to subjects and objects and employing a simple access control rule for each access authorization. Using boolean expressions to achieve exact access patterns from subjects to objects is more precise in reflecting the security needs of practical applications, since in the real world, the relationships among subjects for accessing objects often can be expressed appropriately by the language of boolean algebra. Furthermore, this model is extended from a stateless model to a more powerful version in which states are associated with subjects and objects simply by dividing their security attributes into two classes and rendering different meanings to different classes in access authorization. A controlled attribute updating rule is designed to reflect the change of security attributes due to accesses. Done this way, the overhead of implementing states on system entities can be reduced to the minimum.

As demonstrated earlier, the modeling power of the *BEAC* model is surprisingly great. All security policies which can be enforced by a lattice-based multilevel security model are only a proper subset of all the security policies that can be enforced by *BEAC*. In addition, many desirable access control policies which cannot be adequately enforced by either a conventional multilevel model or the access control matrix model, such as multilevel exceptions and access sequence, can be effectively enforced by the model. As a nice property, the basic techniques for the enforcement of simple policies can be combined further to enforce more complex security policies. The model has also been implemented as a client-server access control system using C language, with high-level remote procedure calls as the communication mechanism between clients and the server.

In the near future, more modeling power of *BEAC* should be explored, i.e., more complex security policies applicable to the model should be investigated. There exist many imminent works in the implementation of *BEAC*. A policy-to-mechanism translation system can be built to facilitate specification of security policies. Thus, a *policy specification language* needs to be designed and implemented to allow the user to specify various security policies. The translation system then needs to convert appropriately a policy into security attributes of subjects and objects. The current realization of *BEAC* puts all attribute management under the access control server. A more practical implementation for distributed systems should store security attributes of subjects under the management space of subjects.

6.3 Access Control with Extended Capabilities

An extended capability system is introduced to model complex access control policies in distributed systems. The strategy is to augment the functions of traditional capabilities such that security requirements need not be enforced by centralized access control lists. In this *E-cap* system, tedious and complicated access control information is translated into an *ACI* field in the capability by the access control server and distributed to the subjects by the object server. The object server is only required to keep simple capability processing rules and well-designed enforcement mechanisms. When a capability is presented for accessing an object, the object server makes an authorization decision by invoking proper processing rules based on the *ACI* information on the capability. It has been demonstrated that many complex security policies can be enforced elegantly in a decentralized manner with efficiency both in time and storage. The methodology for distributing all capabilities for a security policy at a time is also different from the conventional way of distributing capabilities on demand. It is believed the former way will render performance advantage over the latter since the communication overhead with the access control server is minimized.

Possible future works include completion of the specification of the ACI field such that all major security policies can be encompassed and structurally represented, and support of capability revocation more selectively and efficiently.

REFERENCES

[1] Martin Abadi, Michael Burrows, Charles Kaufman, and Butler Lampson, *Authentication and Delegation with Smard-cards*, DEC SRC Research Report 67, October 1990.

[2] Martin Abadi and Roger Needham, *Prudent Engineering Practice for Cryptographic Protocols*, DEC SRC Research Report 125, June 1994.

[3] G. T. Almes, A. P. Black, E. D. Lazowska, and J. D. Noe, "The Eden System: A Technical Review," *IEEE Transactions on Software Engineering*, Vol. SE-11, No. 1, January 1985, pp. 43 – 59.

[4] Paul Ammann, Ravi Sandhu, and Gurpreet Suri, "A Distributed Implementation of the Extended Schematic Protection Model," *Proceedings of the 7th Annual Computer Security Applications Conference*, San Antonio TX, December 1991, pp. 152 – 164.

[5] Jean Bacon, Richard Hayton, Sai Lai, and Ken Moody, "Extensible Access Control for a Hierarchy of Servers," *ACM Operating Systems Review*, Vol. 28, No. 3, July 1994, pp. 4 – 15.

[6] Lee Badger, "A Model for Specifying Multi-Granularity Integrity Policies," *Proceedings of the IEEE Symposium on Security and Privacy*, Oakland, CA, May 1989, pp. 269 – 277.

[7] David E. Bell and Leonard J. LaPadula, "Computer Security Model: Unified Exposition and Multics Interpretation," Technical Report ESDTR-75-306, The MITRE Corporation, Bedford, MA, June 1975.

[8] Steven M. Bellovin and Michael Merritt, "Limitations of the Kerberos Authentication System," *Proceedings of the Winter 1991 Usenix Conferences*, Dallas, TX, February 1991, pp. 1 – 15.

[9] Kenneth J. Biba, "Integrity Considerations for Secure Computer Systems," Technical Report ESDTR-76-372, The MITRE Corporation, Bedford, MA, April 1977.

[10] Ray Bird, Inder Gopal, Amir Herzberg, Philippe Janson, Shay Kutten, Refik Molva, and Moti Yung, "Systematic Design of a Family of Attack-Resistant Authentication Protocols," *IEEE Journal on Selected Areas in Communications*, Vol. 11, No. 5, June 1993, pp. 679 – 693.

[11] W. E. Boebert, "On the Inability of an Unmodified Capability Machine to Enforce The *-Property," *Proceedings of the 7th DoD/NBS Computer Security Conference*, Washington, D.C., September 1984, pp. 291 – 293.

[12] David F. C. Brewer and Michael J. Nash, "The Chinese Wall Security Policy," *Proceedings of the IEEE Symposium on Security and Privacy*, Oakland, CA, May 1989, pp. 206 – 214.

[13] Michael Burrows, Martin Abadi, Roger Needham, *A Logic of Authentication*, DEC SRC Research Report 39, February 1990.

[14] Leslie S. Chalmers, "A Analysis of the Differences between the Computer Security Practices in the Military and Private Sectors," *Proceedings of the IEEE Symposium on Security and Privacy*, Oakland, CA, April 1986, pp. 71 – 74.

[15] David D. Clark and David R. Wilson, "A Comparison of Commercial and Military Computer Security Policies," *Proceedings of the IEEE Symposium on Security and Privacy*, Oakland, CA, April 1987, pp. 184 – 194.

[16] Robert Cole, "Some Issues in Security Arising from Distribution," *Proceedings of the Workshop on Operating Systems of the 90s and Beyond*, Dagstuhl Castle, Germany, July 1991, pp. 202 – 206.

[17] F. Cuppens, "A Logical Analysis of Authorized and Prohibited Information Flows," *Proceedings of the IEEE Symposium on Research in Security and Privacy*, Oakland, CA, May 1993, pp. 100 – 109.

[18] David A. Curry, "Improving the Security of Your Unix System," Technical Report ITSTD-721-FR-90-21, SRI International, April 90.

[19] Dorothy E. Denning, "A Lattice Model of Secure Information Flow," *Communications of the ACM*, Vol 19, No. 5, May 1976, pp. 236 – 243.

[20] Dorothy E. Denning, *Cryptography and Data Security*, Addison-Wesley, Readings, MA, 1983.

[21] Dorothy E. Denning and Giovanni Maria Sacco, "Timestamps in Key Distribution Protocols," *Communications of the ACM*, Vol. 24, No. 8, August 1981, pp. 533 – 536.

[22] Jack B. Dennis and Earl C. Van Horn, "Programming Semantics for Multiprogrammed Computations," *Communications of the ACM*, Vol. 9, No. 3, March 1966, pp. 143 – 155.

[23] Whitfield Diffie, Paul Van Oorschot, and Michael Wiener, "Authentication and Authenticated Key Exchanges," *Design, Codes and Cryptography*, Vol. 2, No. 2, June 1992, pp. 107 – 125.

[24] Deborah D. Downs, Jerzy R. Rub, Kenneth C. Kung, and Carole S. Jordan, "Issues in Discretionary Access Control," *Proceedings of the 1985 IEEE Symposium on Security and Privacy*, Oakland, CA, April 1985, pp. 208 – 218.

[25] Deborah Estrin, "Inter-organization Networks: Implications of Access Control Requirements for Inter-connection Protocols," *Computer Communications Review*, Vol. 16, No. 3, August 1986, pp. 255 – 264.

[26] Deborah Estrin, Jeffrey Mogul, and Gene Tsudik, "*Visa* Protocols for Controling Interorganizational Datagram Flow," *IEEE Journal on Selected Areas in Communications*, Vol. 7, No. 4, May 1989, pp. 486 – 498.

[27] Todd Fine and Spencer E. Minear "Assuring Distributed Trusted Mach," *Proceedings of the IEEE Symposium on Research in Security and Privacy*, Oakland, CA, May 1993, pp. 206 – 218.

[28] Simon N. Foley, "A Taxonomy for Information Flow Policies and Models," *Proceedings of the IEEE Symposium on Research in Security and Privacy*, Oakland, CA, May 1991, pp. 98 – 108.

[29] Li Gong, "On Security in Capability-Based Systems," *ACM Operating Systems Review*, Vol. 23, No. 2, April 1989, pp. 56 – 60.

[30] Li Gong, "A Secure Identity-Based Capability System," *Proceedings of the IEEE Symposium on Security and Privacy*, Oakland, CA, May 1989, pp. 56 – 63.

[31] Li Gong, "A Security Risk of Depending on Synchronized Clocks," *Operating Systems review*, Vol. 26, No. 1, January 1992, pp. 49 – 53.

[32] Li Gong, "Lower Bounds on Messages and Rounds for Network Authentication Protocols," *Proceedings of the 1st ACM Conference on Computer and Communications Security*, Fairfax, Virginia, November 1993, pp. 26 – 37.

[33] Li Gong, Roger Needham, and Raphael Yahalom, "Reasoning about Belief in Cryptographic Protocols," *Proceedings of the IEEE Symposium on Security and Privacy*, Oakland, California, May 1993, pp. 234 – 248.

[34] L. Gong, T. M. A. Lomas, R. Needham, and J. H. Saltzer, "Protecting Poorly Chosen Secrets from Guessing Attacks," *IEEE Journal on Selected Areas in Communication*, Vol. 11, No. 5, June 1993, pp. 648 – 656.

[35] Andrzej Goscinski, *Distributed Operating Systems: The Logical Design*, Addison-Wesley, Reading, MA, 1991.

[36] F. T. Grampp and R. H. Morris, "UNIX Operating System Security," *AT&T Bell Laboratories Technical Journal*, Vol. 63, No. 8, October 1984, pp. 1649 – 1672.

[37] Michael A. Harrison, Walter L. Ruzzo, and Jeffrey D. Ullman, "Protection in Operating Systems," *Communications of the ACM*, Vol 19, No. 8. August 1976, pp. 461 – 471.

[38] Information Processing Systems - Open Systems Interconnection - The Directory - Authentication Framework, ISO/IEC 9594-8, CCITT 1988 Recommendation X.509, 1988.

[39] Robert R. Jueneman, "Integrity Controls for Military and Commercial Applications," *Proceedings of the 4th Aerospace Computer Security Application Conference*, Orlando, FL, December 1988, pp. 298 – 322.

[40] Richard Y. Kain and Carl E. Landwehr, "On Access Checking in Capability-Based Systems," *Proceedings of the IEEE Symposium on Security and Privacy*, Oakland, CA, April 1986, pp. 95 – 100.

[41] I-Lung Kao and Randy Chow, "An Efficient and Secure Authentication Protocol Using Uncertified Keys," *Proceedings of the 2nd Annual Workshop on Selected Areas in Cryptography*, Ottawa, Canada, May 1995, pp. 49 – 56.

[42] I-Lung Kao and Randy Chow, "Enforcing Complex Security Policies for Commercial Applications," to appear in *Proceedings of the 19th Annual International Computer Software and Applications Conference*, Dallas, TX, August 1995.

[43] I-Lung Kao and Randy Chow, "Enforcement of Complex Security Policies with BEAC," to appear in *Proceedings of the 18th National Information Systems Security Conference*, Baltimore, MD, October 1995.

[44] I-Lung Kao and Randy Chow, "An Extended Capability System for Enforcement of Complex Security Policies in Distributed Systems," submitted to the *5th IFIP Working Conference on Dependable Computing for Critical Applications*.

[45] Paul A. Karger, "The Lattice Security Model in a Public Computing Network," *Proceedings of 1978 ACM Annual Conference*, Washington, D.C., December 1988, pp. 453 – 459.

[46] Paul A. Karger, "Implementing Commercial Data Integrity with Secure Capabilities," *Proceedings of the IEEE Symposium on Security and Privacy*, Oakland, CA, May 1988, pp. 130 – 139.

[47] Paul A. Karger and Andrew J. Herbert, "An Augmented Capability Architecture to Support Lattice Security and Traceability of Access," *Proceedings of the IEEE Symposium on Security and Privacy*, Oakland, CA, April 1984, pp. 2 – 12.

[48] Paul A. Karger, Mary E. Zurko, Douglas W. Bonin, Andrew H. Mason, and Clifford E. Kahn, "A VMM Security Kernel for the VAX Architecture," *Proceedings of the IEEE Symposium on Research in Security and Privacy*, Oakland, CA, May 1990, pp. 2 – 19.

[49] A. Kehne, J. Schonwalder, and H. Langendorfer, "A Nonce-Based Protocol for Multiple Authentication," *Operating Systems review*, Vol. 26, No. 4, October 1992, pp. 84 – 89.

[50] Bulter W. Lampson, "Protection," *Proceedings of the 5th Princeton Symposium on Information Sciences and Systems*, Princeton, NJ, March 1971, pp. 437 – 443.

[51] Carl E. Landwehr, "Formal Models for Computer Security," *Computing Surveys*, Vol. 13, No. 3, September 1981, pp. 247 – 278.

[52] Theodore M. P. Lee, "Using Mandatory Integrity to Enforce Commercial Security," *Proceedings of the IEEE Symposium on Security and Privacy*, Oakland, CA, April 1988, pp. 140 – 146.

[53] H. M. Levy, *Capability-Based Computer Systems*, Digital Press, Bedford, MA, 1984.

[54] Armin Liebl, "Authentication in Distributed Systems: A Bibliography," *ACM Operating Systems Review*, Vol. 27, No. 4, October 1993, pp. 31 – 41.

[55] Barbara Liskov, "Practical Uses of Synchronized Clocks in Distributed Systems," *Proceedings of the Tenth Annual ACM Symposium on Principles of Distributed Computing*, Montreal, Quebec, Canada, August 1991, pp. 1 – 9.

[56] Teresa F. Lunt, "Aggregation and Inference: Facts and Fallacies," *Proceedings of the IEEE Symposium on Security and Privacy*, Oakland, CA, May 1989, pp. 102 – 109.

[57] Catherine Meadows, "Extending the Brewer-Nash Model to a Multilevel Context," *Proceedings of the IEEE Symposium on Research in Security and Privacy*, Oakland, CA, May 1990, pp. 95 – 102.

[58] Dale A. Moir, "An Implementation of Access Control Using a Salient Feature of Primes," *Proceedings of the 7th Annual Computer Security Applications Conference*, San Antonio, TX, December 1991, pp. 298 – 322.

[59] Refik Molva, Gene Tsudik, Els Van Herreweghen, and Stefano Zatti, "KryptoKnight Authentication and Key Distribution System," *Proceedings of 1992 European Symposium on Research in Computer Security*, Toulouse, France, November 1992. pp. 1 – 16.

[60] Michael J. Nash and Keith R. Poland, "Some Conundrums Concerning Separation of Duty," *Proceedings of the IEEE Symposium on Research in Security and Privacy*, Oakland, CA, May 1990, pp. 201 – 207.

[61] National Computer Security Center, "Department of Defense Trusted Computer System Evaluation Criteria," DoD 5200.28-STD, December 1985.

[62] Roger M. Needham and Michael D. Schroeder, "Using Encryption for Authentication in Large Network of Computers," *Communications of the ACM*, Vol. 21, No. 12, December 1978, pp. 993 - 999.

[63] Roger M. Needham and Michael D. Schroeder, "Authentication Revisited," *Operating Systems Review*, Vol. 21, No. 1, January 1987, p. 7.

[64] D. M. Nessett, "Factors Affecting Distributed System Security," *Proceedings of the IEEE Symposium on Security and Privacy*, Oakland, CA, May 1986, pp. 204 – 222.

[65] B. Clifford Neuman and Stuart G. Stubblebine, "A Note on the Use of Timestamps as Nonces," *Operating Systems review*, Vol. 27, No. 2, April 1993, pp. 10 – 14.

[66] E. I. Organick, *The Multics System: An Examination of its Structure*, MIT Press, Cambridge, MA, 1972.

[67] Dave Otway and Owen Rees, "Efficient and Timely Mutual Authentication," *Operating Systems Review*, Vol. 21, No. 1, January 1987, pp. 8 - 10.

[68] Charles P. Pfleeger, *Security in Computing*, Prentice Hall, Englewood Cliffs, NJ, 1989.

[69] F. Piessens, B. De Decker, and P. Janson, "Interconnecting Domains with Heterogenerous Key Distribution and Authentication Protocols," *Proceedings of the IEEE Symposium on Research in Security and Privacy*, Oakland, CA, May 1993, pp. 66 – 79.

[70] R. F. Rashid, "Experiences with the Accent Network Operating System," *Networking in Open Systems: International Seminar*, Oberlech, Austria, August 1986, pp. 259 - 269.

[71] R. F. Rashid, "Mach: A New Foundation for Multiprocessor Systems Development," *IEEE COMPCON'87 — Digest of Papers*, 1986, pp 192 - 193.

[72] Ravi Sandhu, "Transaction Control Expressions for Separation of Duties," *Proceedings of the 4th Aerospace Computer Security Application Conference*, Orlando, FL, December 1988, pp. 282 - 286.

[73] Ravi S. Sandhu and Gurpreet S. Suri, "A Distributed Implementation of The Transform Model," *Proceedings of the 14th National Computer Security Conference*, Washington, D.C., October 1991, pp. 177 - 187.

[74] William R. Shockley, "Implementing The Clark/Wilson Integrity Policy Using Current Technology," *Proceedings of the 11th National Computer Security Conference*, Baltimore, MD, October 1988, pp. 29 - 37.

[75] Abraham Silberschatz and Peter B. Galvin, *Operating System Concepts*, 4th Edition, Addison-Wesley, Reading, MA, 1994.

[76] Lawrence Snyder, "Formal Model of Capability-Based Protection Systems," *IEEE Transactions on Computers*, Vol. C-30, No. 3, March 1981, pp. 172 – 181.

[77] Jennifer G. Steiner, Clifford Neuman, and Jeffrey I. Schiller, "Kerberos: An Authentication Service for Open Network Systems," *Proceedings of the Winter 1988 Usenix Conference*, Dallas, TX, February 1988, pp. 191 – 201.

[78] Daniel F. Sterne, "On the Buzzword "Security Policy"," *Proceedings of the IEEE Symposium on Research in Security and Privacy*, Oakland, CA, May 1991, pp. 219 – 230.

[79] Paul Syverson, "On Key Distribution Protocols for Repeated Authentication," *Operating Systems Review*, Vol. 27, No. 4, October 1993, pp. 24 - 30.

[80] Andrew S. Tanenbaum, Sape J. Mullender, and Robbert van Renesse, "Using Sparse Capabilities in a Distributed Operating Systems," *Proceedings of the 6th International Conference on Distributed Computing Systems*, Cambridge, MA, May 1986, pp. 558 – 563.

[81] Victor L. Voydock and Stephen T. Kent, "Security Mechanisms in High-Level Network Protocols," *ACM Computing Surveys*, Vol. 15, No. 2, June 1983, pp. 135 – 171.

[82] Raymond M. Wong, "Issues in Secure Distributed Operating System Design," *Proceedings of the 34th Annual IEEE International Computer Conference*, San Francisco, CA, February 1989, pp. 338 – 341.

[83] W. Wulf, R. Levin, and S. Harbison, "HYDRA: The Kernel of a Multiprocessor Operating System," *Communications of the ACM*, Vol. 17, No. 2, February 1974, pp. 337 – 345.

[84] Raphael Yahalom, *A Logic of Authentication*, DEC SRC Research Report 39, February 1990.

BIOGRAPHICAL SKETCH

I-Lung Kao was born on June 12, 1964, at Taipei, Taiwan, Republic of China. He graduated from National Taiwan University with a Bachelor of Science degree in agricultural machinery engineering in June, 1986. After working in the Taiwan's largest research institute for about a year, he entered the Department of Mechanical Engineering at the University of Michigan in September, 1987, and received his first Master of Science degree in December, 1988. He started his graduate study in computer and information science and engineering at the University of Florida in January, 1989, and obtained his second Master of Science degree in May, 1991. He will obtain his Doctor of Philosophy degree in August, 1995.

I certify that I have read this study and that in my opinion it conforms to acceptable standards of scholarly presentation and is fully adequate, in scope and quality, as a dissertation for the degree of Doctor of Philosophy.

Randy Y. C. Chow, Chairman
Professor of Computer and Information
Science and Engineering

I certify that I have read this study and that in my opinion it conforms to acceptable standards of scholarly presentation and is fully adequate, in scope and quality, as a dissertation for the degree of Doctor of Philosophy.

Paul A. Fishwick
Associate Professor of Computer and
Information Science and Engineering

I certify that I have read this study and that in my opinion it conforms to acceptable standards of scholarly presentation and is fully adequate, in scope and quality, as a dissertation for the degree of Doctor of Philosophy.

Richard E. Newman-Wolfe
Assistant Professor of Computer and
Information Science and Engineering

I certify that I have read this study and that in my opinion it conforms to acceptable standards of scholarly presentation and is fully adequate, in scope and quality, as a dissertation for the degree of Doctor of Philosophy.

Jih-Kwon Peir
Associate Professor of Computer and
Information Science and Engineering

I certify that I have read this study and that in my opinion it conforms to acceptable standards of scholarly presentation and is fully adequate, in scope and quality, as a dissertation for the degree of Doctor of Philosophy.

Samuel B. Trickey
Professor of Physics and of Chemistry

This dissertation was submitted to the Graduate Faculty of the College of Engineering and to the Graduate School and was accepted as partial fulfillment of the requirements for the degree of Doctor of Philosophy.

August 1995

Winfred M. Phillips
Dean, College of Engineering

Karen A. Holbrook
Dean, Graduate School

www.ingramcontent.com/pod-product-compliance
Lightning Source LLC
Chambersburg PA
CBHW080428060326
40689CB00019B/4428